BOOM & BUST
IN BONE VALLEY

IN BONE VALLEY

FLORIDA'S PHOSPHATE MINING HISTORY 1886-2021
AND THE LOOMING ECOLOGICAL CRISIS

TED EHMANN

SHOTWELL
COLUMBIA · SO. CAR.
EST. 2015
PUBLISHING

Produced in the Republic of South Carolina by

SHOTWELL PUBLISHING LLC
Post Office Box 2592
Columbia, So. Carolina 29202

www.ShotwellPublishing.com

Cover Image: Hand mining phosphate 1900. State Archives of Florida, floridamemory.com

ISBN 978-1-947660-55-7

10 9 8 7 6 5 4 3 2 1

To Wendell Berry, a uniquely American voice and our most eloquent witness to the damage to our farmlands and to our communities. To Kirkpatrick Sale, who reminds us of our limits as humans and instructs us to live within those limits, and to those of you who wish to nurture the land, the people and our shared existence.

TABLE OF CONTENTS

PREFACE

I conceive a strip-miner to be a model exploiter, and as a model nurturer I take the old- fashioned idea or ideal of a farmer. The exploiter is a specialist, an expert; the nurturer is not. The standard of the exploiter is efficiency; the standard of the nurturer is care. The exploiter's goal is money, profit; the nurturer's goal is health- his land's health, his own, his family's, his community's, his country's.

Wendell Berry

P.1 Lonesome palms, wetlands and a vast sky in the Florida interior, Florida Department E.P.A.

In Southwest Florida, once you leave Highway 41 or Interstate 75 and drive east into the interior, you literally enter another world. At first glance, you are overwhelmed by the sameness of the terrain and fauna that make up this interior. With hardly a light or a stop sign for the next two hours till you reach the Atlantic coast, you can drive so fast that it is easy not to notice what makes the interior so special when compared to the coastal environs. The roads there are cut through the flat wilderness in straight lines, but life in this interior flows in serpentine rivers and streams; a primary system is the Peace River (P.2) and the creeks that feed it. There are lakes there, as well, like gems that break the sameness of these lands. Finally, you begin to slow a bit, moving at the pace that is the pace of the interior region. You pause and take in the endless sky, a sky free of any viewing obstacles save a few lonely palm trees (P.1). Drive further, and eventually you will see the scarred terrain of former phosphate mining. Make a wrong turn you may even up in an active mining area. You are in Bone Valley.

Generations of fossil hunters know well the beauty and the rhythm of theses interior lands and the Peace River Valley, for you have to step into the water and become a part of it all to feel the fossils on the bottom of the river and the creeks with your bare feet. Every now and then finding through touch the rock-hardened remains of prehistoric giants who saw humans as food some 14,000 years ago. In the Peace River the prehistory and the geology is tangible and accessible. It is a lot different from taking your kids to view them behind glass in a museum. (P.3)

They also know, more than others, how the area was made useless and uninhabitable by decades of strip mining. Ghost towns appear in the distance, like the lonely smoke stack (P.4), where the busy mining town and plant of Brewster once stood (P.5).

It is said that, necessity is the mother of invention. In the mid-nineteenth century, soils used for agriculture were depleted of vital nutrients by decades of exploitation and poor farming methods. The search was on for a solution. Trial and error on the European continent resulted in the discovery of phosphate mineral resources to restore the soil's fertility. The solution was 100% natural, but like its cousin fossil fuels, phosphate pebbles and rock

P.2 Peace River, Shutterstock

*P.3 Children view prehistoric animals at the Mulberry Phosphate Museum,
1950s Florida Department of State*

P.4 Old smoke stack for Brewster phosphate power plant, Wikimedia.com

P.5 Brewster phosphate plant 1950s, Florida Department of State

deposits need sulphuric acid to dissolve it, and the resource is not renewable. There are also sizable environmental risks associated with the mining of phosphate. The search for deposits of phosphate rock took on a life of its own as early as the 1870s, in the Deep South, beginning in the Lowlands around Charleston, S.C. So valuable was this new mineral, it was referred to as 'gray gold.' You cannot view the various episodes of phosphate mining, without likening them to the prior gold rush in California. Most people, however, are unaware that by all accounts and by every measure, phosphate mining is still a boom industry in Florida today. At of the writing of this history, the world's largest producer of phosphate for fertilizers and potash, The Mosaic Company, is making strategic mining plans to the year 2050.

The early phase of the phosphate mining boom of the late eighteen- hundreds in the Florida's Bone Valley, spanned less than two decades before the turn-of-the-century. Fortunes were made and lost. Mines, railroads and towns sprang up almost overnight. Tracks of land that you could not give away before 1881 were suddenly worth a small fortune. Small fishing ports soon became major industrial centers for exporting phosphate to markets around the world. A rock formed 15 million to 5 million years ago, now a part of the ancient sea bed and forming the central spine of peninsular Florida, by the late nineteenth century was one of civilization's most needed resource. The largest deposits in North America were those found in both the northern and southern veins in Bone Valley. The lower vein is also the entire Peace River Valley, its headwaters in Bartow, Polk County and its bay in Charlotte Harbor on the Gulf Coast. There, in and around the lazy, winding river, is found a wealth of prehistoric fossils lying in rest. The obscure river meandering through it would soon draw the wealthy and less fortunate to its banks. Ever since the eighteen hundred's, the Peace River had been radically transformed by industry and commerce. To the casual reader of history, the phosphate mining boom in Florida was not unlike all the great mining booms. Speculators from all over sought claims in what was and remains wilderness. The creeks and rivers, were the first to give up the precious mineral (P.6). Soon more intensive mining deep into the earth was necessary.

P.6 Phosphate Barge on the Peace River 1905, Florida Department of State

P.7 Bone Valley miners posing in front of their tent homes, Florida Department of State

The miners and their families lived in primitive camps and makeshift towns. It was a hard life (P.7). In Florida, phosphate was discovered in unsettled wilderness. For those who sought to exploit the deposits there, it meant having a life, cut off from anything familiar and anything which could be considered civilized.

At the heart of the mining for 'gray gold' in Bone Valley was agriculture. Agribusiness, even in the nineteenth century, demanded more and more nutrients to replenish the soil. Fertile soil was needed to feed the ever-growing populations of the world. By eighteen sixty-seven, the industrial revolution was in full swing, and so was population growth. In nineteen hundred there were 1.6 billion mouths to feed. By a century later, there were 6.145 billion. Therefore, this history is forever linked to agriculture. This book is about the intersection of two of the greatest revolutions in human history, the agricultural revolution and the industrial revolution. The Deep South, which ended up with the largest reserves of phosphate, needed to save agriculture for generations to come, was at first reluctant to embrace the industrial revolution, preferring their agrarian ways. The South continued to follow the agrarian practices of societies that were used for 3,700 years prior to the industrial revolution. (P.8). The northern cities, however, by the mid nineteenth century seemed to be racing to industry. Their populations moving to towns and cities in order to produce goods and products in the new mechanized world, far removed from home, hearth and native soil.

P.8 Historic photo of farmers at fertilizer store, Smithsonian Archives

At the height of the mining boom before 1900, there were over two-hundred and fifteen mining companies, at least on paper, spanning the 106 miles of the Peace River alone. After 1900, only fifty remained. Today, that number is 6 (the five largest are all owned by one international mining corporation) who currently mine over 15,000 acres in Bone Valley. Late in 2018 another group of speculators and venture capitalists formed HPS Enterprises, a limited liability corporation which is seeking permits to mine in Bradford and Union Counties in northern Florida. That entire northern portion of Bone Valley had been quiet for almost a hundred years. The residents of Bradford are welcoming a company with no history, while residents in Union began fighting the approval on environmental grounds (P.9). This is important, since it is the first time since the end of the nineteenth century that speculators have shown up in phosphate rich Florida. It is also the first time such speculations were met with immediate opposition. It is important to note, that neither Bradford nor Union Counties have been previously mined for phosphate. Therefore, 135 years after the boom started in Florida, mining speculation is still occurring.

P.9 Preserve the Santa Fe River protesters, Photo by Merrillee Malwitz-Jipson.

P.10 Carolina Fertilizer Ad with prehistoric monsters 1890s,
Courtesy of the Charleston Museum

The phosphates for fertilizers global market has grown tremendously because of the exponential increase in global population. Most of Mosaic (the largest mining company in Florida and one of the largest in the world) Company's phosphates today are sold to growers of grains used to feed livestock to serve the increased global demand for meat. While there are plentiful sources of phosphate around the world and in the United States in the Deep South, for reasons that I will discuss, phosphate mining has found a willing ally in the politics of Florida. This alliance is now under increasing attacks by environmental groups and everyday residents of Florida.

The new phosphate mining industry in the fossil-rich lowlands of South Carolina, which started the boom in the United States, was short-lived; but the contrasts between the outcomes in both areas are significant and revealing (P.10). Unlike South Carolina, the State of Florida did nothing to control and limit phosphate mining companies. They had a laissez faire approach from day-one. Florida only became involved when the new federally mandated environmental laws forced them to be more proactive. Capitalism brought about the control and dominance of a single company's ownership of Florida's mines. Today, The Mosaic Company's Florida (P.11) mines produce 75% of the U.S. farmer's supply of granular phosphate fertilizer and 12% of the global supply. The most recent figures on tonnage are from Reuters in 2013. Mosaic's mines shipped 7.5 million tons of phosphate crop nutrients and 15 million tons of phosphate rock. Of the 15,000 employees worldwide, Mosaic's Florida operations produce one half of those jobs. For all intents and purposes, the boom never left Florida. The economic contributions in terms of wealth and employment are as high, if not higher, than in 1890.

P.11 Mosaic Plant, Peace River, Shutterstock

P.12 Dead fish from red tide on Sanibel Island Beach, August 2018, Shutterstock

What has changed as Florida's phosphate mining industry transitions into another century is opposition. Not just opposition to new mines has increased, but to any and all phosphate mining. In counties down river, environmental groups and watershed organizations are now taking on not only Mosaic's plans to expand their mining operations, but to discourage or stop the mining of phosphates in all of Florida's environmentally fragile environments.

I am writing this history after the second largest and most-deadly outbreak of red tide in Florida's recent history. Since the summer of 2018, the news articles, reports and public meetings in reaction to the crisis that threatens Florida's waterways, wildlife, recreation and tourism blame fertilizers. Nutrients used by agribusinesses feed the algae which cuts off the oxygen in these waters. The Environmental Protection Agency stated recently that nutrient pollution has been responsible for these outbreaks. The federal, state and local governments spend a great deal of money each year to attack this new problem. In 2016, forty years after an accident that destroyed the Peace River ecology for generations, (P.12) citizens forced DeSoto County to reject phosphate giant Mosaic Company's plan for an additional 17,000 acre mine. Somehow the true cost for the mining boom in the 1800's was forgotten over time, only to re-emerge in a new age of environmental awareness in the new century. Since 1990 an additional six more dams or berms have failed in the Bone Valley. Nutrient pollution is a whole other issue from phosphate mining operations and mining accidents. In Florida the two issues have been collapsed into one, which is threatening the health Florida's residents as well as the now fragile tourism and real estate industries. To date, there are not enough studies that would link phosphate and phosphate fertilizers to the outbreaks of red tide in southwest Florida (P.12).

The mining of phosphates and the fortunes made by a few in that process is an on-going history, which has allowed me a history with relevancy. Many respectable scientists and naturalists recently have emphasized the very fragile ecology in Florida. The truth is that all the eco-systems of the world are fragile. Without nutrients like phosphates to restore the life of the growing fields of the world, there simply will not be enough crops to feed the population of the world. Multi-national mining concerns pay millions to reclaim the lands after strip mining, but accidents happen. Most effects from such accidents have been irreversible. For many Floridians, it appears that the cost they are asked to bear are two-fold. First there is the degradation of the watershed and aquifers from accidents due to mining. Second is the loss of healthy and productive lands and the failure to restore the ecology.

If a good story has a conflict, the story of phosphate mining is currently ripe with conflict. That it has taken all these years to reach this inevitable fight is part of the history. Florida has reached the point where the status quo is more risky than to change course.

People in Florida, it appears, will play a role in the future of phosphate mining, making a reliable history important in order that they may make more informed decisions. Every year, tourist visit the Mulberry Phosphate Museum in Bone Valley. Originally a large private collection of fossils, in 1986, it was decided to create a museum that chronicled the history of phosphate mining. Upon visiting the museum, you get a nostalgic view of the once great industry. There are no exhibits that educate the public on the cost to the environment, and the potential looming ecological crisis. Nearby are sites which truly show the wealth and power of phosphate mining in Florida's Bone Valley, such as the elegant mansions and 1908 Courthouse in downtown Bartow. The courthouse, now an Historical Center, rivals the State House in Tallahassee. If you haven't visited, do so. Sure, the cattle business had a great deal to do with the rise of Bartow, but phosphate mining made the county's achievements unprecedented and grand. The mansions and grand decorative courthouse also stand in stark contrast to the ghost towns throughout the valley.

My attempt here is to tell the entire story of the people, places and events; not just past but present. My function as researcher and historian is not to take sides, but rather to tell the complete story from multiple perspectives. There are good reasons to look at the present and even the future through the lessons of the past. All resources are limited. As the world population approaches the 8 billion mark, there are many reasons to listen to the people who are left with ecological disasters, the consequences of industry without limits. I am haunted by the words of Wendell Berry, published some forty-four years ago, that the strip-miner was to him the "model exploiter." After 135 years of phosphate mining, will enough, be enough?

1.1 19th Century etching of chemistry laboratory, Alamy

I.

MEN OF INDUSTRY AND SCIENCE AND THE INDUSTRIALIZATION OF AGRICULTURE

Historians Marcel Mazoyer and Laurence Roudart, in *A History of World Agriculture*, describe how the first agricultural revolution began in the sixteenth century. Farmers devised systems, without fallowing, to create surplus crops. The surplus resulted in time free from farming. The free time allowed men to pursue science and commerce.[1] (1.1) How we take that dramatic shift for granted. It took untold millennia for individuals to just provide for their families and just as many years for individuals to have time to do more than just live hand-to-mouth.

> In American history, no one exemplifies a man of industry, science and intellectual pursuit more than Thomas Jefferson (1.2). Jefferson not only ran a successful plantation in Virginia, but in his free time, studied and commented on everything from philosophy to the natural sciences. His instruct to "question with boldness even the existence of god,"[2] is a testimony to his belief in a free and open-minded pursuit of knowledge. How easily we all forget that it was changes in how Europeans farmed that allowed the middle-class the time and resources to pursue their research and make discoveries.

Though there are differing accounts of the discovery of using high-grade phosphate pebbles and rock for agriculture, the credit should go to German chemistry professor Justus Von Liebig (1803-

1.2 Portrait of Thomas Jefferson,
Courtesy of Virginia Museum of History

1.3 Portrait of Justus Von Liebig,
Wikimedia.com

1873) (1.3). Referred to by many as the father of modern chemistry, as well as the father of the fertilizer industry, he started everything. Von Liebig researched the production and use of "chemical manures" in 1845. His absolute concept of only inorganic nutrient uptake by plants was obviously inaccurate, yet it has persisted in modern soils literature. This represents a case of mechanistic rigidity in the history of science that illustrates a lack of a functional understanding of natural systems.

I believe a statement made by Kirkpatrick Sale (1.4) in his book, *Human Scale*, sums it up:

> And there is nothing but the shortest step from this sense of separateness to the complete state of hubris that assumes that there is nothing humans can do, that science can do, that they should not do, because the natural world is essentially there for our benefit.[3]

1.4 Portrait of author Kirkpatrick Sale,
Courtesy of author

While Von Liebig's work was not effective, his research into chemicals for fertilizer ultimately led to the rendering of certain minerals for use in plant food.[4] His work was the critical research that formed the basis for the modern fertilizer industry. This use of chemistry would play a critical role in South Carolina, and eventually in the Bone Valley.

The boom and bust in the late 1800's in the Bone Valley would also not have been possible without the work of French naturalist Pierre Berthier (1782-1861). It was who discovered the presence of phosphate of lime in nodular form[5] and recognized its importance. This knowledge, through research and experimentation, soon led to the scientific understanding of manufacturing fertilizers from phosphate[6] in Europe. It was Berthier who found that phosphate could be dissolved with sulphuric acid. Therefore, by as early as the late 1840's, men of industry and science knew how to test phosphate nodules and process them, and saw their great potential and value as a commercial fertilizer.

Chemist would continue to bring the critical understanding of chemical properties to advance the ideas for new fertilizers. In 1856, a Charleston, South Carolina physician Dr. St. Julien Ravenel (1.5) partnered with chemist Clement H. Stevens in a commercial venture mining lime from his plantation on the Cooper River. Ravenel was not a disciplined, scientific chemist. He made no records of his observations and experiments. A rather solitary, reserved and private person, Ravenel was strictly business. Fortunately, we have hundreds of his letters to his wife and the lawyers later involved in his Wando Fertilizer Company. In 1866, his Wando company was the first recorded commercial phosphate concern established in the United States without "foreign capital." That was no small thing, since it was the critical needs in Europe that drove the discovery of and the eventual manufacturing of phosphates for fertilizers.

Ravenel was revered at the time. Upon Ravenel's death, there was a special *Proceedings of The Agricultural Society of South Carolina* on April 13.1882. It was a very emotional memorial to Dr. Ravenel. During those proceedings, it was stated that Ravenel had "urged the rigid adherence to two principles of agricultural economy, not generally observed among us, name: to plant no

1.5 Drawing of St. Julien Ravenel's home, Charleston S.C., Courtesy of Charleston Museum

more land than can be cultivated thoroughly, and to manure thoroughly,"[7] manure being generic to any fertilizer. Next the writer of the proceedings, addressed Ravenel's work with fertilizers in the context of agriculture in the South after the Civil War.

> Wise as is the practice of these principles always, conformity with them in our poverty and with expensive labor was a necessity. It was easier of course to plant one instead of two or three, or more acres, but whence were to come the manures to make their reduced acreage adequately productive, without money to buy them abroad and with our resources for making them at home crippled our sheep, our cattle, our horses and mules, greatly reduced by the war and what remained of them depredated on and all but destroyed in the lawlessness of the times.[8]

To understand this statement is to understand the Deep South that gave birth to the boom and the bust to follow.

1.6 Specimen of mineral phosphorite or rock phosphate, Aleksandr Pobedinsky

After the Civil War, Ravenel left the general practice of medicine and cloistered himself in research, especially in chemistry. One can surmise that he played a significant role in the money-producing events in Beaufort County, South Carolina. At that time, rather than scientific exploits, it does appear that his interests were driven entirely by financial benefits after the defeats of the Civil War. He researched and wrote about the needs of farmers and for scientific agriculture. The third individual responsible for the phosphate boom was Dr. N.A. Pratt. His personal history, except for his involvement with Ravenel, is unknown. Research has provided no biographical data on Dr. Pratt. His actions and role as the catalyst for the phosphate epoch in South Carolina indicate that he was not a wealthy southerner from a noted family. He was an entrepreneur, who was the first individual to see the significance and great financial rewards in phosphate-based fertilizers, a major contribution in the long run. Therefore, in terms of the "discovery of the commercial value of" and the mining of phosphates for fertilizer in the Deep South, the credit goes to Dr. N.A. Pratt, as well as Dr. St. Julien Ravenel. Both independently and simultaneously commercialized their findings. Without them there would not have been mining boom and just a museum filled paleontological specimens (1.6) in Bartow would celebrate Florida's Bone Valley, otherwise just worthless wilderness land.

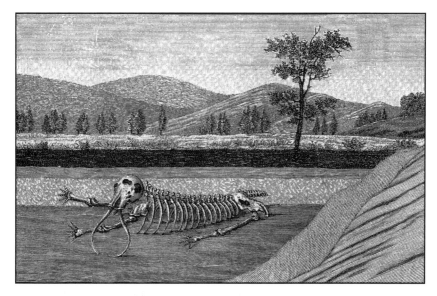

1.7 18th Century etching of a fossil find, Alamy

An associate of Ravenel in Charleston, in fact the man with the cases filled with fossils (1.7), Francis S. Holmes, was the only man of industry and science in the South Carolina lowlands who conducted his research and applied it to agriculture. A self-educated paleontologist, before his death, Holmes actually wrote about farming and in his own way was an early dabbler in scientific-based farming methods.[9] Previous histories give him too much credit for the phosphate mining epoch which followed. History clearly shows that it was the money men, the doers and not the thinkers, who brought phosphate mining to the Deep South, and eventually to Florida.

There has always been an intense interest in the major human revolutions, because they changed every aspect of life on this planet. The history of phosphate mining in Florida and the earlier chapter in the South Carolina lowlands are the intersection of industrialized mining with global food production, two major revolutions.. With the projected population growth of the earth in view, the subject could not be more relevant.

In the 1990s, in response to a book by Kirkpatrick Sale entitled *Dwellers In the Land: The Bioregional Vision,*[10] many, especially in the then Green Movement went into action along with its author Kirkpatrick

Sale, defining the bioregion where they lived. For this author, the findings and future research became a series of bioregional festivals. The second festival on sustainable agriculture was held at Rudolph Steiner-based Camp Hill community in Kimberton, Pennsylvania.[11] Over the year of planning, organizers became knowledgeable about the profound relationships between healthy farming and healthy communities. Such views have been labeled as utopian, even though as we discovered, they were the norm for 32,500 years. At the very heart of issues regarding agriculture and community is the question of scale. Sustainability has been on the side of localized and smaller scale farming. Non-sustainability increases with the larger, less-localized and centralized agricultural practices. What caused the massive shift was an emphasis on "economics".

The imprint on farming, communities and even culture by the scientific/ industrial paradigm has been profound. While mineral phosphates such as pebbles and rock are found in nature, they are not easily dissolved in water by natural processes. Consequently, from an ecological viewpoint, mineral phosphate deposits are not part of the phosphorus cycle that exists in nature, assisting in the growth of organisms. Being an inorganic fertilizer, phosphates have been part of the use of chemicals in industrialized agriculture. This is because inorganic fertilizers are generally less expensive and have higher concentrations of nutrients than organic fertilizers. Also, since nitrogen, phosphorus and potassium generally must be in the inorganic forms to be taken up by plants, inorganic fertilizers are generally immediately bioavailable to plants without modification. Slow-release fertilizers may reduce leaching, loss of nutrients and may make the nutrients that they produce available over a longer period of time.

Organic farmers know all-to-well that soil fertility is a complex process, thereby involving the constant cycling of nutrients in both organic and nonorganic forms. As plant material and animal wastes are decomposed by micro-organisms, they release inorganic nutrients into the soil. This process is called mineralization. Plants require and use inorganic forms of nitrogen, phosphorus and potassium (potash), competing for those nutrients. In the end, they are a stored biomass. In 2008, multiple market researchers stated that the cost of phosphorus as fertilizer more than doubled, while the price of phosphate as a base commodity rose eight-fold. Global scarcity of inorganic fertilizers along with increased demand resulted in the term "peak Phosphorus,"[12] which has come to define the limited occurrences of rock phosphate in the world at the end of the twentieth-century. Peak phosphorus will create in the twenty-first century, the potential for a global food security crisis according to author Tariel Morrigan.[13]

Most importantly, small farmers were the heart of civilization. For thousands of years, those small farms were the basis of community and the source of human values and cultures. Communities, based on the natural cycles defined who we were as people (1.9). As author Wendell Berry reminds us therefore, that a crisis in farming was a crisis in community and culture. For thousands of years, there was no concept of large-scale farming, of agricultural as an industry, and especially of farms being owned and farmed by outside interests. That would soon change. The South, more than most regions, was already familiar with market-driven agriculture.

1.8 Advertisement for the Ashley Fertilizer Company 1890s,
Moses 1882 from Michael Trinkley Paper

1.9 Sharecropper family, Courtesy of the Smithsonian Archive

In his signal book on the subject, *The Unsettling of America,* Wendell Berry wrote:

> The soil is the great connector of lives, the source and destination of all. It is the healer and restorer and resurrector, by which disease passes into health, age into youth, death into life. Without proper care for it we can have no community, because without proper care for it we can have no life.[14]

Most of us learned about the agricultural revolution in school. What we didn't learn was that there was, as weely.com refers to it, a second agricultural revolution that gave birth to systems without fallowing. It is impossible to truly understand the phosphate mining boom in the Deep South without understanding the context and the root cause for the making of phosphate based fertilizers. Fallowing was the system of plowing but leaving the field unseeded during the growing system. (1.10). A system of allowing the field to self-fertilize. The Enlightenment Era in Europe gave birth to the natural sciences as well as modern economics. In the old system, grasses and legumes were seeded. Use of manure increased cereal crop yields on un-fallowed fields to such a degree that surpluses were experienced. Soon other crops were planted, those requiring higher fertility. In

1.10 Photograph of fallow field, istock

rapid time the number of livestock and food crops doubled. According to authors Marcel Mozoyer and Laurence Roudart in their A History of World Agriculture, "From the end of the nineteenth century, more than half of the active population in the industrialized countries could devote themselves to rapidly developing nonagricultural activities, such as mining, industry and services."

As a young child I routinely visited farms, feeding their livestock and getting lost in their vast cornfields. Growing up in the north, I also developed the view that farmers were backward people. They lack intelligence and culture, a bias and belief still held by some Americans living in the urban centers. Wendell Berry (1.11) wrote an entire book, *The Unsettling of America,* to call attention to this disconnect in industrialized America between the land and the people, between people and food. Berry finds the origins of this disconnect at the level of the soul or spirit. " The question of human limits, of the proper definition and place of human beings within the order of Creation, finally rests upon our attitude toward our biological existence, the life of the body in this world."[15]

Here, Berry is not only drawing attention to wilderness and nature in general, like some over-zealous environmentalist or naturalist, he is drawing attention to the soil that is the primary connection to the world. "But the questions are also agricultural, for no matter how urban our life, our bodies live by farming, we come from the earth and return to it, and so we live in the particles of the earth, joined inextricably both to the soil and to the bodies of other living creatures."[16]

1.11 Portrait of Kentucky farmer and author Wendell Berry, Courtesy of the author

Ever ask someone, where their food comes from? Most will answer "the store." Ask yourself, for that matter, in 2021. It's difficult to know where what you eat is grown. That has to do with advances in transportation and the existence of global markets. But even as late as 1950, most Americans knew where their food came from, we ate locally and seasonally. We also ate much more healthy and nutritious foods.

Berry wrote that book in the 1970's. Even in 2021, environmental organizations fighting phosphate mining in Florida still do not get it. While fighting against pollution, they fail to acknowledge its connection to how we grow our food, the entire industrial paradigm, not just one piece of the malady. Strip mining, the type of mining used to extract phosphate for fertilizers, is the polar opposite of families and companies living and working within limits, nurturing while extracting life-affirming foods. Proper farming and agriculture are cooperative and nurturing, and for centuries those qualities spilled over into the communities and cultures.

The history of the development of phosphate minerals for soil fertility, from day one, was accomplished by individuals living entirely within the scientific and economic paradigm that had birthed the industrial revolution, and was rapidly replacing the holistic views that had dominated farming for thousands of years. The opposite of disconnected, is connected. Today, we appear to understand all the parts, but after centuries, we are still ignorant of their interrelations and how they work as a whole. Berry beckons us to a conversation about this in relationship to the body and the earth, between the collective body and agriculture. Berry and others have a wisdom, they know that growing food, soil vitality and health cannot be reduced to biology, botany and chemistry. Agriculture, as Sir Albert Howard referred to it, is the "great subject of health in soil, plant, animal and man which has been reduced to fit first the views of a piecemeal 'science' and the purposes of corporate commerce."[17] This was not the case when agriculture consisted of small privately-owned farms, who husband the land with a knowledge and understanding that was only possible by generations of living and working the land. Geography, geology and the life sciences became the tools of commerce, but a commerce that was exploitive. The industrialization of agriculture, today referred to as agribusiness, is 'piecemeal science.'[18] Its goal is profit, not health. The agrichemical companies, such as the ones included in this history, have played a significant role in the industrialization of agriculture. To quote Berry's opening paragraph in *The Unsettling of America* "Once the unknown of geography was mapped, the industrial marketplace became the new frontier, and we continued, with largely the same motives and with increasing haste and anxiety, to displace ourselves."[19] Displacement of people and culture, of all living things, has been the product of both great human revolutions.

That some of the world's richest deposits of rock and pebble phosphate were found in former Confederate states, did not bode well for the futures of those lands. After the Civil war, to quote author Phil Leigh, "Capitalistic moguls became role models and nearly everywhere, outside the South, Americans focused optimistically on the pursuit of wealth." The new economic possibilities of gaining from the Southern losses seemed endless.

One of the worst disasters in world-farming history came about in the United States as a result of the legislated disconnects in several federal land policies. Again, the disastrous results were made possible by the large scale of acres and settlers.

1.12 Family homesteading in Florida 1870s, Florida Department of State

Just before the Civil War, the United States Congress passed The Homestead Act of 1862.[20] The law provided incentives to would-be settlers (1.12) that included 160 acres of public lands for each settler. Passage of the Kincaid Act[21] in 1904, and in 1909 the Enlarged Homestead Act, led to large tracts of previously unfarmed lands to be farmed by completely inexperienced farmers. (1.13) In the Great Plains, rising wheat prices in the 1910s and 1920s, along with increased demand for wheat from Europe during World War I encouraged farmers to plow up millions of acres of native grassland to plant wheat, corn and other row crops.

For all the years prior to 1910 the average farm size in the United States, per author Mark Shepard, was 138 acres. The average family farm was not mechanized, as Shepard states in his book *Restoration Agriculture*:

> In 1910, there were 6.4 million farms in the United States. Most farms were owned by the farmer and his family, back then more farmers were male. The

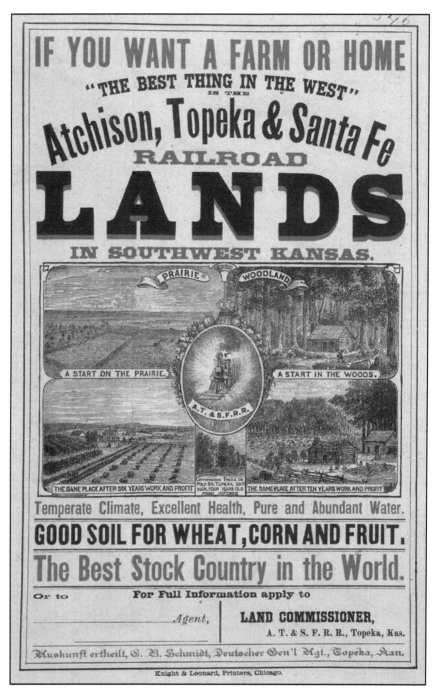

1.13 Poster advertising lands to be homesteaded, U.S. Senate

1.14 Lithograph, New England Farm, Thomas Hart Benton,
Courtesy of Black Rock Galleries

small family farms provided a modest but healthy livelihood for its inhabitants which were typically large extended families. (1.14)

What occurred in farming after 1910 was nothing less than a revolution. Similar to the dramatic decline of phosphate mining companies and consolidation in the fertilizer production, the number of farms in the United States went from 6.4 million to 2.2 million in the next 100 years. By 2008, the average American farm size was 461 acres. None of this would have been possible without the invention of the tractor and the shift to fossil fuels.

Over-speculation led the financial crash in 1929. We all know the history of the Great Depression that lasted so many years as the government intervened with policies that hurt and exasperated the problems. Farmers grabbed larger tracts of unfarmed acres in an attempt to produce bumper crops in order to simply break even. In the Great Plains, the drought which began in 1931 dried the top soil and the wind then carried it away. (1.15)

Seeking to settle the new frontier, with no knowledge of the land, we became unsettled in the very process and damaged the land. Wendell Berry refers to the term "kindly use."[22] All land use, including farming, involves living on the land, a connection to and

15

*1.15 Photograph, Deserted Farm Dust Bowl, Dorothea Lange,
Library of Congress*

thus a knowledge of the land. Use of lands by strangers, be they individuals, corporations or governments can never be kindly, for all of those generalize the land. He stated:

> To treat every field, or every part of every field, with the same consideration is not farming, but rather industry. Kindly use of land, depends upon intimate knowledge, the most sensitive responsiveness and responsibility. Knowledge when generalized, the essential values that are good land management are destroyed.[23]

The growing of annual crops requires the removal of an intact perennial ecosystem, like the native grasses that protected the soils in the Great Plains and elsewhere. The soil must be tilled in order to seed. Immediately the soil is exposed. Little by little, the precious fertile soil is compromised and removed by rain and wind. Since the agricultural revolution circa 3500 B.C., farmers knew that in order to secure the fertility of their field, nature required that fields lay fallow between crops. The economic pressures following the industrial revolution created such competition that these natural practices were abandoned. The first to experience the dramatic changes resulting from the industrial revolution were the Europeans. It was the new practices that resulted in the use of and reliance on chemical fertilizers. It was the market that was responsible for the hunt for gray gold in the southeastern United States.

It follows that alternative methods to farming, focused on restorative means, would come out of Europe. In 1924, Rudolph Steiner of Germany, advanced the very first "organic" agriculture movement. Steiner's approach treated soil fertility, plant growth and livestock care as "ecological interrelated tasks." His methods were called biodynamic farming and from my experience with these communities in the United States, composting is raised to a spiritual level. He viewed the farm and production as a single system.[24] A hundred percent natural approach, chemical fertilizers were replaced by the manure and compost that was the mainstay of farming for 5,400 years.

Another father of the modern organic farming methods was Great Britain's Sir Albert Howard. Born in 1873, the son of a farmer, Howard ended up in India. His observations became embodied in his *An Agricultural Testament.*[25] Howard observed and came to support traditional Indian farming practices over conventional scientific agriculture. He had journeyed to India to teach Western agricultural techniques, but he found that the Indians could in fact teach him more. One important aspect he took notice of was the connection between healthy soil and the villages' healthy populations, livestock and crop. Patrick Holden quoted Howard as saying "the health of soil, plant, animal and man is one and indivisible." Howard was president of the thirteenth session of the Indian Science Congress in 1926.[26]

After Steiner and Howard, another approach, permaculture was developed. It was yet another restorative form of agriculture, not only restorative to farming but to the relationships between agriculture and community. A leading voice has been Mark Shepard. Shepard (2013) talks about the advent of chemical nitrogen fertilizers thus:

had a short-lived boom on yields, but instead of improving the bottom line for farmers, they had the opposite effect. More crops meant lower prices. Fertility which once came from livestock raised on farms, now came in a bag from the Agri-chemical company down the road. In less than a lifetime, farms went from being self-contained ecological production systems, to debt-ridden, input dependent "agri-businesses" that soon required massive government subsidies to keep them afloat.[27]

Sir Albert Howard, during the eve of World War II, delivered a wake-up call to the governments and the peoples of the world. He was the miner's canary on the state of soil erosion, soil infertility and their relationship to poor nutrition, health and disease. Howard's statistics revealed that as of 1937, in the United States, "no less than 253,000,000 acres, or 61% of the total area under crops, had either been partly destroyed or had lost most of its fertility." The first U.S. president to sound the alarm was Teddy Roosevelt fifty years prior. While agricultural lands increased dramatically during the Gilded Age, so too did soil erosion and disease. Today, we think nothing unusual about the growing number of organic growers. The permaculture movement,[28] which is nothing less than a complete turn-around to the old systems, supported by the rational conclusions of Albert Howard and the others, is gaining in credibility. Eliot Coleman, a leader in the movement and author, wrote recently in his book, *The New Organic Grower*:

> The only truly dependable production technologies are those that are sustainable over the long term. By that very definition, they must avoid erosion, pollution, environmental degradation, and resource waste. Any rational food-production system will emphasize the well-being of the soil-air-water biosphere, the creatures which inhabit it, and the human beings who depend upon it.[29]

In my preface, I spoke of the uproar due to the lingering red tide in Florida. Stated earlier, the average farm acreage dramatically increased in the past 100 years. So too did the use of chemical fertilizers. Florida residents believe that they know the causes of the outbreaks of red tide on the southwest coast of Florida. More and more, Florida residents are calling attention to biosphere issues, the big picture as it relates to the role of fertilizers in environmental degradation. At a public meeting with an overflow of people attending in Englewood, Florida in 2018, marine biologists tried to sell the public on the idea that red tides are part of the natural system. (1.16) Organic farmers like Eliot Coleman and Mark Shepard know the truth of the matter about this unintended consequence of the reliance on chemical fertilizers. He also addresses what happens when riparian buffers are not present in agricultural areas. Mark Shepherd wrote:

> Agricultural chemicals, especially costly fertilizers soak into roots on the riparian buffer, and no longer travel the streams that feed the Mississippi River down to the Gulf of Mexico (and help enlarge the dead zone). One of the main causes of the hypoxic dead zone in the Gulf of Mexico is the overfertilization of the ocean caused by the agricultural runoff...[30]

The red tide that plaques south Florida today is man-made.

Recently a spokesperson for the phosphate industry told a reporter at an event in Tampa to basically back-off of negative press on Florida's phosphate mining. He repeated the same belief promoted in agri-business today, that without the chemical fertilizers, the populations in the world will go hungry.[31] The situation is much more complex than he related. Proponents of change emphasize the culture inherent in agriculture. Their concerns are for sustainable and healthy food production, the ecology that includes human societies. It cannot be reduced to putting something in your stomach.

1.16 Hardee County citrus growers,1900s, Florida Department of State

Regarding soil quality, Florida passed a law and a tax on phosphate mining companies in 1975, requiring full reclamation of mined lands. Besides cattle ranching, many of the lands in the Bone Valley have been agricultural lands. There is no history, and thus no adequate research and knowledge about returning to say citrus growing on lands that have been reclaimed. Mosaic has been conducting their own testing and have led officials and the public to believe that after former agricultural acres have been mined, it is fairly easy to return the land to growing and agriculture. It is a fool's errand.

The independent research conducted on the latest mining expansion by Mosaic in Hardee County, an area with a history of citrus growing in the state disputes Mosaic's bold claims. A June 6, 2002 suitability study told the commissioners that reclaimed land with soils that have high concentrations of clays and phosphate from the mining lack permeability.[32]

Permeability is an essential soil quality for roots and watering of planted trees and crops. Despite studies showing the county that they would give up all chances to agricultural use of the lands after the mining, they went ahead and approved the plans.

Returning to the insights of folks like Albert Howard and Wendell Berry, places like the former agricultural communities of Hardee County lose their community, their culture, and enter a future of uncertainty and loss.

In my first book on prehistoric Florida, *People of the Great Circle,* I turned to a technique for investigating a given subject by bringing in voices, who though they never provided insights to the particular topic, offer invaluable perspective and insight, when inserted into the new discussion. Wendell Berry never wrote a single word about the phosphate boom in the Bone Valley, nor has historian Kirkpatrick Sale. Upon my completing this study, their voices had become critical and indispensable. No matter where my research went, their voices kept me from getting lost and losing sight of what this history tells us about us and our relationship to the land.

Endnotes

1 Mazoyer and Rodardt, 2006

2 Thomas Jefferson, Paris, Letter to Peter Carr, August, 1787

3 Kirkpatrick Sale, 2000

4 Felschow, Eva-Marie. *"Justus Liebig (our Eponym),"* Justus Liebig University. (Retrieved 5 November 2014)

5 *Ibid.*

6 en.wikipedia.org/wiki/Pierre_Berthier

7 *Proceedings of The Agricultural Society of South Carolina* on April 13, 1882.

8 *Proceedings of The Agricultural Society of South Carolina* on April 13, 1882.

9 Lester Stephens, www.scencyclopedia.org/sce/entries/holmes-francis-simmons/

10 Kirkpatrick Sale, 2000

11 www.camphillkimberton.org/special-needs-community/

12 Tariel Morrigan, *Peak Phosporus, A Potential Food Security Crisis,* http://climateproject.global.ucsb.edu/publications/pdf/Morrigan_2010_Peak%20Phosphorus.pdf

13 *Ibid.*

14 Wendell Berry, 2015

15 *Ibid.*

16 *Ibid.*

17 Albert Howard, 1940

18 http://www.fao.org/3/am361e/am361e.pdf

19 Wendell Berry, 2015

20 https://www.archives.gov/education/lessons/homestead-act

21 Todd Arrington, https://www.archives.gov/education/lessons/homestead-act

[22] Wendell Berry, 2015

[23] *Ibid.*

[24] https://en.wikipedia.org/wiki/Biodynamic_agriculture

[25] Albert Howard, 1940

[26] *Ibid.*

[27] Mark Shephard, 2013

[28] https://permacultureprinciples.com/

[29] Eliot Coleman, 2018

[30] baysoundings.com/legacy-archives/sum05/phosphate6.html

[31] https://www.fool.com/investing/general/2013/03/20/mosaic-enters-phosphate-joint-venture-in-saudi-ara.aspx

[32] https://www.marketwatch.com/press-release/the-mosaic-company-reports-third-quarter-2019-results-2019-11-04

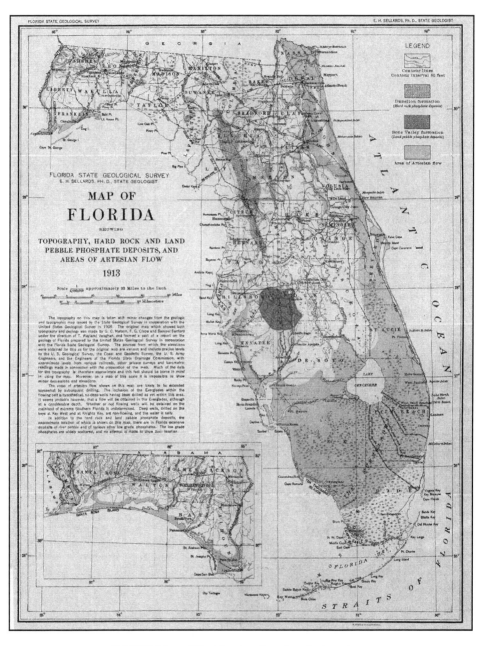

*2.1 1913 Map of Florida, showing phosphate regions,
Florida Department of State*

II.

IT'S IN THE MIX,
THE MINING OF PHOSPHATE

Unlike the events that would be unfolding in nearby Florida, phosphate mining in South Carolina was conducted in a relatively small area, the rivers in the lowlands encircling Charleston. Discovered in these river beds were the phosphate pebbles. But the mining boom there, as stated before, was short lived. South Carolina's losses soon became Florida's gains. During the brief decades when phosphate was king in South Carolina's lowlands, the first phosphate mining companies in the Deep South spent considerable capital developing the phosphate mining processes and advances in equipment needed to extract phosphate rock, process, transport and store it.

The history of phosphate mining in the Deep South is difficult to fully understand, without a basic understanding of how phosphate is mined and processed. This understanding becomes critical when I discuss phosphate mining, accidents and lawsuits that have been a part of the history from the twentieth century to today.

In order to fully understand the history of phosphate mining in Florida, one in which I include present and future mining, it is necessary to understand a little bit about the origins of the phosphate deposits in Florida's Bone Valley. I believe that the public will find such knowledge, not only useful, but critical for dealing with the fallout of 135 years of phosphate mining on the Florida peninsula. (2.1)

The geology of Florida's phosphate reserves has been the primary factor in the state's phosphate mining because, even to today, mining companies must have easy access to higher grade phosphate in order to economically mine the mineral (2.2).

2.2 Swift Mine, Bone Valley, 1920s, Florida Department of State

Florida's vast deposits of phosphate pebbles and hard rock came into being due to earth forces that occurred during the Miocene, a geological epoch that was 23 to 5 million years ago.[1] The particular formation where the phosphate resides is called the Hawthorn Group Formation (2.3). Florida geologists Anthony Randazzo and Douglas Jones wrote:

> Formation and preservation of large phosphorite deposits are made possible by a relatively rare combination of tectonic settings, climate, sea level and oceanic circulation.[2]

Therefore, for as long as we have known about these geological epochs in the twentieth century, we have been aware that these reserves are rare. This fact was unknown in the early days of phosphate mining. Randazzo and Jones state further that a large influx of organic matter to sediment, required to form phosphate was limited to regions of upswelling ocean water. They conclude that " To form phosphate the organic matter must make it to the

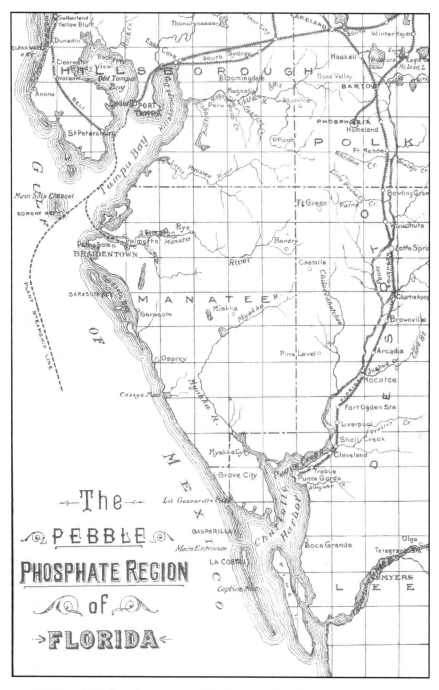

2.3 The pebble phosphate region of Florida map. Florida Department of State

sea floor."[3] In Florida, we have known that there is much variety in phosphate grain size, indicating that Florida's phosphorites had several and not just one origin.[4]

Critical to understanding the history of phosphate mining in Florida is to know the different "zones," each zone indicating a different origin.[5] The main phosphate ore zone has been the Peace River Formation in the Hawthorn Group, known as Bone Valley. Geographically these deposits are in Polk and Hillsborough Counties (2.4). These deposits are believed to have been deposited in a warm shallow sea in a sea-shore environment according to Riggs, 1984. Riggs refers to the region as a "mix zone" since it is primarily iron-aluminum phosphate.[6] According to Randazzo and Jones, 1997: "Technology and economics allowed the miners to move from the river pebbles to the land and the hard rock and finally mining the finer-grained phosphate matrix." [7]

Essentially, the Florida phosphate matrix is a mixture of clay, quartz, sand, dolomite and phosphates. In the previous chapter, I discussed Wendell Berry's distinction regarding kindly vs. generalized use of land in farming. My reference to Florida's phosphate matrix is

2.4 19th century photo of mining town of Fort Mead looking over the mining pits, Florida Department of State

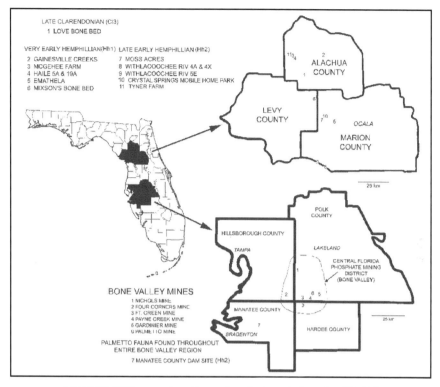

LATE CLARENDONIAN (Cl3)
1 LOVE BONE BED

VERY EARLY HEMPHILLIAN(Hh1) LATE EARLY HEMPHILLIAN (Hh2)

2 GAINESVILLE CREEKS   7 MOSS ACRES
3 MCGEHEE FARM   8 WITHLACOOCHEE RIV 4A & 4X
4 HAILE 5A & 19A   9 WITHLACOOCHEE RIV 5E
5 EMATHELA   10 CRYSTAL SPRINGS MOBILE HOME PARK
6 MIXSON'S BONE BED   11 TYNER FARM

ALACHUA COUNTY

LEVY COUNTY

MARION COUNTY

OCALA

25 km

POLK COUNTY

HILLSBOROUGH COUNTY

TAMPA

LAKELAND

CENTRAL FLORIDA PHOSPHATE MINING DISTRICT (BONE VALLEY)

MANATEE COUNTY

BRADENTON

HARDEE COUNTY

25 km

BONE VALLEY MINES

1 NICHOLS MINE
2 FOUR CORNERS MINE
3 FT. GREEN MINE
4 PAYNE CREEK MINE
5 GARDINER MINE
6 PALMETTO MINE

PALMETTO FAUNA FOUND THROUGHOUT ENTIRE BONE VALLEY REGION

7 MANATEE COUNTY DAM SITE (Hh2)

2.5 USGS 1930 map of northern phosphate rock deposits, U.S.G.S.

a generalized view. Phosphate mining is relatively simple, and even simpler and more profitable in the phosphate matrix of Bone Valley, accounting for its long history there.

In Chapter VII, I will discuss the efforts by the one remaining phosphate mining company to begin mining in the Southern Extension Zone Bone Valley, in Manatee, DeSoto and Hardee Counties. Owing to five characteristics of the zone, mining companies have been in no rush to mine these reserves.[8] The depletion of the more economically beneficial deposits in Polk and Hillsborough Counties have made this a last-ditch effort. The five characteristics present in the zone that have resulted in delayed mining efforts are: more marine facies, lower PO, high MgO, higher overburden to ore ratio and leached zone ores. One leach zone ore, of great concern to environmentalists, is the high content of uranium.[9]

The third Florida zone has been referred to as the hard rock district. The history of Florida's gray gold starts in this region. Deemed to be technically and economically less-desirable, except for a small amount of mining today in Hamilton County, all hard rock mining ceased in the 1960's. The zone of hard rock reserves is vast and covers the following northern Florida counties: Alachua, Citrus, Dixie, Gilchrist, Hernando, Lafayette, Levy, Marion, Sumter and Taylor counties according the USGS.[10] (2.5)

Historically the mining of this rare mineral has been relatively simple. Even in the earlier days of phosphate mining it involved primarily labor and simple extracting, washing, drying and processing technologies. By the late 1890's the steam engine helped to increase production of river and land pebble mining, as well as hard rock (2.6) (2.7).

The invention of the dragline revolutionized phosphate mining by the 1920's. For the past 100 years, phosphate mining consists of: preparing the land, removing the overburden by the dragline, and mining the ore by the same dragline (2.8)(2.9). The ore is dropped into pits and then slurred (2.10). Finally, this slurry is pumped to the mineral processing plant (2.11). For that reason, as long as there is availability and a good market value for the mineral, Florida phosphate mining has been very profitable.

From the earliest geological studies to the twenty-first century, it has been learned that Florida's phosphate zones and deposits are anything but simple. Within a single zone, even within a single mine there can be a great deal of variety; variety in the composition and concentration of phosphate, and variety in the other minerals that make up the matrix.[11] For the geologists, all the data is interesting and revealing. For the

2.9 Miner riding in dragline bucket 1920s, Florida Department of State

2.6 Steam-driven shovel, Bone Valley, Florida Department of State

2.7 Steam-driven mining barge, Dunnellon, Florida Department of State

2.8 Dragline, Bone Valley, Florida Department of State

2.10 Miners piping water to make slurry, Florida Department of State

2.11 Processing Plant 1930s, Florida Department of State

2.12 Two miners with picks and shovels 1890s Dunnellon, Florida Department of State

companies which view each subset of knowledge, the decisions can be daunting. With each variation there is either economic benefit or liability.

By 1997, Florida led the world in the production of phosphate rock. While some geologists like W.F. Stowasser predicted as much as a 20% increase in phosphate production by the year 2000,[12] the majority of experts from the United States Geological Survey 1997 study and the U.S. Bureau of Mines have predicted a steady decline during the twenty-first century and the termination of phosphate mining by 2010. All eyes now look to Morocco, which has 75% of the remaining minable phosphate reserves.[13]

Sedimentary phosphate tends to be found in loose sediment, so it was mined with picks and shovels (2.12). In South Carolina and then Florida, the phosphate was found mainly in one layer of clay and sand that was about 10-20 feet thick, and 15-50 feet below the surface.[14] After the overburden (the sediment above the desired layer) was dug out by people or later by heavy equipment, they removed and dumped the phosphate-rich sediment into a pit. That sediment then was mixed with water. Today pumps are used

2.13 Slurry and pipeline, Florida Department of State

to pressurize the water to make a slurry (2.13), and that slurry containing phosphate is sent through miles of pipeline. Making and pressurizing the slurry today, requires a lot of electricity (2.14) as well as water. [15]

Recycling of the process water in the nineteenth century was not a consideration. Today by Florida's standards, 95% of water is supposed to be reused.[16] The Florida Industrial Phosphate Research Institute (FIPR) describes on their website the important beneficiation process

Beneficiation has been the necessary process that begins the process of removing the clay mixed with the phosphate mineral.[17] In the first decades, like the extraction, this was done by laborers who crushed, washed and cleaned the clay and sand from the phosphate. Today, the fast movement of the slurry causes it to bang against the pipes, and this breaks apart any clay balls. What arrives at the beneficiation plant are fine-grained sand, clay and phosphate sediments suspended in water. At the beneficiation plant, the slurry is first run through a screen, which filters out the coarser sand. To separate the phosphate from the clay, different equipment causes the finer-grained particles to separate from the coarser grains. Finally, a process called flotation is used to separate the phosphate from smaller grained sand. In this process, the phosphate is then coated with a hydrocarbon. When bubbles move through the liquid, the coated particles attach to the bubbles and rise to the surface. This can be done a second time, but using a different hydrocarbon to attach to the sand.[18]

At this point, the sand, clay and phosphate have been separated. The sand and overburden are used to help reclaim land (fill mine pits). Because it remains soggy for a long time, the clay is more of a problem. The clay is spread out over the land. After 3-5 years a solid crust will exist on the clay, but underneath the clay will be soft and pudding-like. Many chemicals toxic to the land and water are in these ponds. Accidents from breached ponds with resulting dispersal into creeks, rivers and bays have resulted during hurricanes and heavy rainfalls, common in Florida. Sinkhole accidents related to ponds have become more common (2.15). The limestone beneath

2.14 Agricola power plant 1910, Florida Department of State

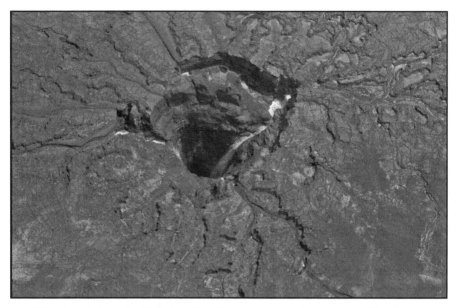

2.15 Giant sinkhole at the Mulberry phosphate plant waste facility, 2016. Florida Department of Enviromental Protection

these pits is continually dissolving by water, a natural process. But the weight of the pits, ponds and overburden can exacerbate the problem, causing a cave-in and allowing the toxic sludge to empty into the aquifer.[19]

Processing of the phosphate into applicable fertilizer during the first several decades of the industry, was done elsewhere, except for a very few companies that both mined and processed it.[20]

Beginning in the twentieth century, the Bone Valley phosphate was sent to a chemical processing plant, or fertilizer manufacturing plant. Here, molten sulfur, shipped to Florida ports and trucked to the plant, was used to create sulfuric acid. The sulfuric acid is then mixed with the phosphate to make phosphoric acid. The phosphoric acid is the main ingredient in fertilizer, but can also be used in animal feed supplements, soda, or soap. Sulfuric acid production creates a lot of heat. This heat is used by a power plant to generate electricity, which helps to power both sulfuric acid production and phosphoric acid production. The mixing of sulfuric acid and phosphate creates gypsum (called phosphogypsum) as a byproduct. Although gypsum can be used for a variety of purposes, the EPA prevents usage of Florida's phosphogypsum because it retains low levels of radioactivity found in the host sediments. At present, phosphogypsum is piled up around the processing plant. Wastewater is also produced. Much is reused, but some fills ponds at the tops of gypsum stacks where water evaporates.[21] Leaks continue to occur in these ponds. Toxic and unsightly gypsum stacks have come to be a symbol of the increased opposition to the expanding phosphate mining in Florida by environmental groups and the public.[22]

Now in the mix, so to speak, are the decades of large scale strip mining. The toxic waste ponds, the gypstacks (2.16), breaches, sinkholes, as well as the push back by environmentalists and the public are now in the mix. A perfect example of this was the recent approval for the mining expansion in Hardee County, Florida, conditional on Hillsborough county taking all the waste there.[23]

2.16 Gypstacks at old mining area, Mulberry, Florida Department of State

ENDNOTES

[1] www.fipr.state.fl.us/about-us/phosphate-primer/fossils

[2] Randazzo and Jones, *The Geology of Florida*, 1997

[3] *Ibid.*

[4] prehistoric florida.org, prehistoricflorida.org/phosphate-and-how-florida-was-forme

[5] floridadep.gov/.../content/phosphate

[6] S.R.Riggs, *The Geology of Florida*, 1997, 64-67

[7] Randazzo and Jones, *The Geology of Florida*, 1997

[8] www.fipr.state.fl.us/publication/characterization-o

[9] https://protectpeaceriver.org/2012/04/uranium-mining-in-va-looks-at-fl-phosphate-recor

[10] https://pubs.usgs.gov/bul/1118/report.pdf

[11] https://pubs.usgs.gov/bul/0934/report.pdf

[12] W.F. Stowasser, *The Geology of Florida*, 1997, 141,143

[13] http://energyskeptic.com/2016/phosphate-production-and-depletion/

[14] www.fipr.state.fl.us/about-us/phosphate-primer/phosphate-beneficiation/

[15] *Ibid.*

[16] d32ogoqmya1dw8.cloudfront.net/files/integrate/...

[17] W.F. Stowasser, *The Geology of Florida*, 1997, 141,143

[18] https://www.sciencedirect.com/science/article/abs/pii/S0892687503001316

[19] https://flmines.com/florida-sinkholes-created-by-phosphate-mining.html

[20] https://en.wikipedia.org/wiki/Boca_Grande,_Florida

[21] *Ibid.*

[22] https://www.sierraclub.org/sites/www.sierraclub.org/files/sce/florida-chapter/documents/PhosphateBro-web.pdf

[23] https://www.tampabay.com/news/breaking/hillsborough-to-be-a-dumping-ground-for-clay-from-hardee-phosphate-mine-

3.1 Two fossil hunters pose with their mastodon jaws, 1950s,
Florida Department of State

3.2 Postcard 1900s Phosphate Mining, Bone Valley,
Florida Department of State

III.

THE MANY GRAY AREAS

The European demand for high grade phosphates for fertilizers which began in the 1840's and sparked the mining boom in South Carolina by 1868, was bigger than ever in 1876, when phosphates were identified in Alachua and Levy Counties, Florida. Dr. C.A. Simmons had begun primitive mining operations and the United States Geologic Survey had reported phosphates in that area as early as 1882.[1] News, at least accounts read by the average Floridian, about the phosphate mining boom in Charleston, never reached the public in Florida. Another fertilizer story in the Pacific Ocean off South America, likewise got no press at the time. Referred to as the Guano Wars, between 1879 and 1884, Chile and Bolivia, newly formed countries, actually went to war over highly marketable nitrate rich guano deposits on a series of islands in the region.[2]

The men of industry and science that birthed the phosphate boom in Charleston over a decade earlier, were followed by primarily men of commerce in the epoch that followed in Florida. To say that Florida was primitive when compared to Charleston and Beaufort County, South Carolina, would be an understatement. There were no great plantations in the area where phosphates were discovered in Florida. Correspondingly, there were few freed slaves living nearby, available for labor. The one river, the Peace River, was far from major commercial centers and rail transportation. People and supplies took a long time getting to and from these remote agricultural outposts. The people of Florida were certainly not ready for the immediate needs that resulted from intense mining of phosphates. Once the word got out, there was no way to contain things. The newly formed state, lacking all required infrastructure, agencies and services, had no way of regulating and inspecting the industry.

In 1881, J. Francis LeBaron, while working for the Army Corp of Engineers, discovered phosphorus pebbles in the Peace River, just south of Fort Meade in rural Polk County, Florida. He was not there to look for gray gold. He was there surveying for a potential canal that would link the St. Johns River with the Great Tampa Bay on the Gulf west coast.[3] While research has yet to uncover his familiarity with and interest in the mineral, especially phosphate's increasing demand for use in industrial fertilizers, he had to be familiar with the phosphate boom already in progress in Charleston. That is to say, by 1881, LeBaron must have known of the mineral's perceived value.[4]

The Peace River is one of those amazingly long rivers with multiple tributaries that snakes through central Florida, then empties into Charlotte Harbor between Port Charlotte and Punta Gorda on the southwestern Gulf coast. No pun intended, but it was only natural that phosphorus rock should be found along the Peace River. Similar to the early fossil finds in New Jersey, the formations beneath the Peace River lie on the great Gulf of Mexico Coastal Plain that begins in Texas and ends in New Jersey, and is known for its fossils.[5](3.1). You could say that where there were fossils, there was phosphate. That is why the entire Peace River Valley was referred to as "Bone Valley." No different from the discoveries in the rivers surrounding Charleston, phosphate pebbles gave rise to land speculators and more aggressive mining (3.2).

The commercial value of phosphate first depended on the percentage of fossilized bone in the rock. The higher the content, the higher the demand. A high grade of commercial phosphate had an 80% plus amount of bone phosphate lime content.[6] Next was the deposition of rock, and last, and particular to mining phosphates in Florida, was the amount of overburden covering the deposits (3.3). All the deposits in South Carolina were exposed. In Florida, we know from the early mining in Dunnellon that the average deposits were at depths from 10 to 20 feet, and overburdened with sand, soil and clays (3.4). Many a fortune was lost in Florida, if after buying large tracts of land one or more of these factors ruined future prospects for mining.

3.3 Mined area with the overburden taken away 1920s, Florida Department of State

3.4 Mining crew starting to dig test pit, 1890s, Florida Department of State

T.D. Allman remarked in his history *Finding Florida:*

> Until then, the scrublands of central Florida were considered good for nothing but grazing cattle. Florida's limestone structure made both temperate and tropical commercial agriculture unprofitable... One of limestone's many avatars is phosphate: immense quantities of it underlie central Florida. Phosphate has two remarkable, indeed paradoxical, qualities. Nothing can grow on it, and nothing can grow without it.[7]

This very astute statement is somewhat tongue in cheek. What grows on the Bone Valley phosphate is the result of co-evolution. What grows there has been dependent on many factors and as such represents each area's unique ecology. If nothing can grow on the Bone Valley deposits, its discovery, like the deposits found in the South Carolina Lowlands would have been a very easy exercise. That was not the case. The deposits in Florida, unlike the Lowlands, are buried. Prospecting for phosphate in Florida began with a sounding rod. A twenty- foot long steal rod was inserted and if it brought to the surface elements of phosphate rock, test pits were dug. The four by six feet pits were dug through the overburden to the rock, and deeper, in order to determine the thickness of the layer. Often fifty-foot long trenches were done in exploration (3.5). Chemists were employed, and often were investors and partners. Verification of the grade of phosphate could make or break you. One of Augustus Vogt's mines went under, when a chemist misread the results.[8] Because of the many feet of overburden, miners using pick and shovel, had to remove all of it and create refuse piles away from the mine. After the rock was exposed, it was removed and put on conveyer belts, where laborers had to remove all impurities by hand.

Florida after the Civil War was intent on returning to the old South. Florida was a slave state and early to secede from the Union. It was their crops and cattle that help support the Confederate troops. Florida also supplied a disproportionate number of troops. Before the war, the total population of Florida was 140,424 and 61,745 slaves. In 1870, the entire population of whites and freedmen

3.5 Public Lynching of Rubin Stacy, July 19, 1935 Fort Lauderdale,
Courtesy of The Shumburg Center

were only 187,748.[9] Unlike Charleston or Atlanta, there were no conversations about a "New South" for Florida that encouraged industry, mills and mining. Land was and had always been dirt cheap. When phosphate was discovered near Dunnellon in 1889, the area was remote with few roads and no infrastructure. Except for the early farmers who had cast their lots, western Florida was the frontier. In short, it was not Charleston or Beaufort County, South Carolina. Prior to the Civil War, Charleston was a large city in the United States. The few towns in frontier Florida had only a dozen or so residents. There were no schools, no churches, no stores and very little law and order. J. Lester Dinkins recounts:

> The first three-year period of 1889 -1891 witnessed the formation of no less than twenty phosphate companies in the immediate Dunnellon area.[10] They estimated that these early mines in that little area alone were capitalized at over $21,000,000.[11] A sign of things to come in Florida, this is the number of mining companies and capitalization for the whole Beaufort County phosphate epoch. Dunnellon grew into a frontier mining camp overnight. By 1894, they were building stores, schools and churches (3.6). African-American men in their twenties descended in large numbers from Alabama, Georgia and North Carolina to work the mines for $1.10 a day. In one year's time, the mining town of Rockwell's population of 500 black laborers exceeded the population of Dunnellon, one-quarter mile to the South. [12]

As, previously stated, after the war, freed slaves in Florida left, leaving a major labor shortage. In the South Carolina lowlands, the freed slaves stayed and farmed their own lands. Two-thirds of the African-American miners were settled, married and worked both the mining and their farms. Only one-third were immigrants from neighboring states.

As with all the other makeshift mining towns that would sprout between 1889 and 1900, the justice of the peace dealt out justice on a makeshift bench beneath a tree every Monday. Everyone had a gun and used it. Saturday nights were particularly violent due to the large mob rule that was commonplace in these frontier mining towns. Shortly after the town came into existence, two black men were accused of several murders, but they were lynched before they were brought to trial.[13] No different from South Carolina, newspapers continuously reported lynchings. Between 1876

3.6 KKK meeting at the Mulberry Baptist Church 1950s, Florida Department of State

and 1897, Florida newspapers had a total of 456 articles on mob lynchings. That number increased to 7397 in the years between 1898 to 1940. (3.6)

The needs for labor increased significantly in Florida after the war. Bosses sought unsuccessfully to harness the African-American laborers via the old school of fear and intimidation. Nowhere was this more apparent than in Polk County, the center of the phosphate mining of the "Bone Valley" to this present day. The successful three industries north in Charleston were made possible due to better labor relations and racial relations in general. Only William Middleton continually and successively attempted to institute the old system there.

A simple one paragraph account on the front page of the Arcadia newspaper, *The Champion*, dated August 23, 1906,[14] demonstrates the casual acceptance of lynching black men:

> Polk County has had another colored lynching. Those Polk County negroes must be the worst ever or else Polk County white folks must be very excitable.

*3.7 Newspaper illustration 1890s of a black miner
working at night, National Archives*

Due to the lower number of blacks in Florida, the lynching rate was higher by comparison to neighboring states. Historians have stated that a black man in Florida was seven times more likely to be executed by a mob than in the Carolinas. And of the counties in Florida, the mining counties of Polk and Hillsborough had a dark history of such, way into the twentieth century. The Associated Press, published an account on March 14,1921 of an armed mob in Polk County that held up the sheriff and deputies with African American William Bowles in custody for running a speakeasy. The Eagle Lake resident, without trial, was hanged on the spot to a tree on the roadside.[15]

In May 5, 2018, *The Ledger* published an article written by Kimberly C. Moore, entitled: "Lynching, Klan Activity Part of Polk's History," in which she chronicled the brutal history of "Bone Valley," and that being the bones of the tortured and murdered black laborers, executed by mobs:

> But there is another part of that history that goes unspoken in most of their homes- The horrific lynching of black people by some Confederate veterans and their descendants, along with white supremacists in Polk County between 1877 and 1950. In addition, some of those veterans and their descendants formed a local branch of the Ku Klux Klan which marched, burned crosses, harassed and even shot people in Polk County until the 1970's.[16](3.7)

The labor needs of the "New South" spawned many public discussions and debates on the subject of race. As early as December 24, 1879, *The Florida Agriculturalist* addressed an article to the Lake George fruit growers. The article, using statistics, argued that there was nothing in reality to support that white labor cannot endure the climate of Florida. The writer concluded that by all means, the fruit growers should hire Europeans.[17] Years earlier, the state of South Carolina passed a bill to increase immigration from Europe to increase the labor force in that state after the war. Southerners had always felt that the slaves from Africa were uniquely better suited to work in the heat and harsh conditions in the Deep South and Caribbean.[18]

At the beginning of the phosphate mining boom, an article appeared in South Carolina's *The Lancaster Ledger,* Nov. 21, 1867 entitled, *On the Free Negro Labor-Negro Voting*, stating:

> That nothing we can now propose will be able to convert an idle, roving, thriftless, free negro population into the steady, healthy, laboring population that we formerly employed in our fields at the South.[19] (3.8)

3.8 Miners take a break, Florida Department of State

3.9 Colorized postcard of Florida Phosphate mine, Florida Department of State

With the phosphate mining boom in full progress in Florida, an article discouraging the employment of white Europeans appeared in *The Florida Agriculturalist,* on October 4, 1893. The writer challenges the opinions supporting the hiring of Europeans by asking the following questions: "Does the negro hold noisy anarchist mass meetings and defy the civil power? Does he throw bombs? Does he block the wheels of traffic by monster strikes?"[20] The history of phosphate mining in the Deep South clearly shows that during its short and profitable time in Beaufort County, South Carolina, labor for the mines was later primarily local married free blacks who ended up with better hours, wages and housing. In short, a stable and productive work force. Compared with a great number of racially, contracted or forced, predominantly unmarried, young and transient men with less than satisfactory working and living conditions.(3.9)

In 1893, the financial panic took out a good portion of the mining companies and the "Great Freeze" brought down the citrus growers eking out a living in the area.[21] By 1897, phosphate prices had dropped from $25.00 a ton to an all-time low of $6.50 a ton. These downturns resulted in many of the miners and farmers leaving the area.[22] Boom and bust, the phosphate market had fewer players after 1898 and had stabilized, but not enough to make a difference. By then phosphate mining in the "Bone Valley," 120 miles southeast, had really taken off. By 1895, the Dunnellon Phosphate Company, the company that had started the Florida epoch, had closed its operations. Years later with the Crash of 1929, the other phosphates mines in northern Florida were done.

By 1890, Florida boasted their new phosphate mining operations. Colorized postcards featured phosphate mining and Bone Valley was known around the world (3.10). When land speculation reached its height and phosphate rock discoveries were recorded, the Bone Valley phosphate region was determined to be 1.3 million acres.[23] The outstanding survey of Florida phosphate was that by George H. Eldridge in 1890, published in 1892 as a part of the Eleventh Census, Department of the Interior, report on mineral industries. Mr. Eldridge visited Florida for several months in 1890 and again in 1891; subsequently he prepared a map. Eldridge's investigations were made under the United States

Geological Survey. Evidently because his map was made by the Census Bureau, it became lost to Florida operators and only again came to their attention in the 1930's. Mr. Eldridge classified Florida phosphate in three divisions: (1) A hard-rock base extending from Tallahassee to a point south of Dade City in Pasco County, about 200 miles long, averaging 20 miles in width. (2) Land-pebble areas, centering around Jasper in Hamilton County, around Waldo in Alachua County, north of Green Cove Springs in Clay County, north of Leesburg in Sumter and Marion Counties, south of what is now Lakeland (then not even a spot on the map), and (3) an area west of Peace River including portions of Polk, Hillsborough, Manatee, and De Soto Counties.[24]

In 1938, the second study of Florida phosphates appeared in a report by the United States Department of the Interior,[25] which I will describe in detail in Chapter VII. A product of a perceived national crisis in farming and soil fertility, the report was far less scientific and credible than its USGS division surveys.

Finally, in 1942, the USGS published a report on their findings on the Florida phosphate reserves. A scientific study, it gave not only the present (1942) approximation of phosphate reserves and their locations, but also references to the history. They included a map. The 1942 report stated:

> The Bone Valley gravel, which contains the land-pebble phosphates, lies unconformably on the Hawthorn formation, the phosphatic-marl formation that supplied the phosphate to the over-lying formations. The Hawthorn in turn rests unconformably on the Ocala limestone.

Historically, it turned out that the land-pebble phosphates, first mined in Beauford County, South Carolina and then south of Dunnellon along the Peace River, have been the "most important commercial source" of Florida's deposits of gray gold. What was true then, applies today, as Mosaic, the largest single mining concern, races to extend their mining in new areas further south that are rich in the economically viable land-pebbles.

ENDNOTES

[1] www.fipr.state.fl.us/.../discovery-of-phosphate-in-florida

[2] https://www.atlasobscura.com/articles/when-the-western-world-ran-on-guano

[3] prehistoric florida.org, prehistoricflorida.org/phosphate-and-how-florida-was-formed/

[4] *Ibid.*

[5] https://en.wikipedia.org/wiki/Gulf_Coastal_Plain

[6] https://www.rsmm.com/research.htm

[7] T.D. Allman, *Finding Florida,* 2013

[8] Lester Dinkins, *Dunnellon Boom Town in the 1890s,* 1969

[9] www.census-online.com/links/FL/1870.htm

[10] Lester Dinkins, *Dunnellon Boom Town in the 1890s,* 1969

[11] https://www.ocala.com/article/LK/20110122/News/604195967/OS

[12] www.census-online.com/links/FL/1870.htm

[13] *Ibid.*

[14] *The Champion,* Arcadia, FL, August 23, 1906

[15] Associated Press, March 14, 1921

[16] Kimberly Moore, *The Ledger,* May 5, 2018

[17] *Ibid.*

[18] *Florida Agriculturalist,* December 24, 1879

[19] *The Lancaster Ledger,* Nov. 21, 1868

[20] *The Florida Agriculturalist,* Oct. 4, 1893

[21] https://en.wikipedia.org/wiki/Financial_panic

[22] *George Eldridge, 1892 Geological Survey, 1892*

[23] *U.S. Department of the Interior 1938 Report on soil fertility*

[24] *George Eldridge, 1892 Geological Survey, 1892*

[25] *Ibid.*

IV.

THE ARRIVAL OF THE RAILROADS AND THE RISE OF THE GULF PORTS

Railroads played the most critical role not only in the populating of the new nation, but in the viability of America's industry. Florida was no exception. A peninsula with water and ports on three sides, the riches from the new phosphate mining were in geological formations in the interior. Mining and shipping phosphate in Florida was not at all like the endeavors during the same boom in Charleston. The rivers where phosphate was discovered and mined in the lowlands of South Carolina flowed into the major shipping port of Charleston for export via the Atlantic shipping lanes to Europe. Thereby, Charleston's mining companies did not have to absorb the cost for rail transportation.

In the mid 1800's Florida was the wilderness. A European colony for centuries, Florida did not become a state until 1845. In contrast, phosphate rich South Carolina, one of the thirteen original colonies, achieved statehood fifty-seven years ahead of Florida. Also, in stark contrast, the venture capitalists in South Carolina were the landed gentry. In Florida, it would be all new money, and northern money at that. The largest populations making a life raising crops or cattle were refugee Indians and escaped slaves from further north or the Caribbean. When Florida became a state in 1845 it had approximately 15 million acres of mostly swamp land.

Congress made grants to states with wetlands for reclaiming land under water.[1] Florida's consolidated grants were put in trust to specifically build rail infrastructure. Florida's Internal Improvement Fund pledged lands to railroad companies and guaranteed bonds issued by railroad companies on their lands.[2] The Civil War and

Reconstruction caused the bonds backed by Confederate dollars to default. To make a long story short, The Trust filed bankruptcy in 1880.[3] Philadelphia born Hamilton Disston, realizing the opportunities, together with five associates approached the State of Florida and eventually, entered into contract to purchase the land for reclamation. In June, 1881, *The New York Times* referred to the transaction as the "largest purchase of land by a single individual in world history."[4]

Keeping my promise to write an inclusive narrative that incorporates the average person who lived through the events, the twelve million acres, albeit wetlands now owned by Disston and his associates, were not uninhabited. His investment threatened to displace untold numbers of squatters. In 1842, Florida passed the Armed Occupation Act in anticipation of its statehood. The act was not intended to remove white families, by granting lands to white squatters, thus, permanently removing thousands of Seminole Indians.[5] The federal troops coming into Florida to remove all of the Indians resulted in the Seminole Wars. It was the longest, bloodiest and most costly Indian conflict in American history.

According to *Florida History.Org*:

> Disston's contract would force the squatters off any land that Disston could show was submerged. The drainage contract, however, was in jeopardy because it did not affect the massive debt bearing down on the Internal Improvement Fund. Court orders related to the debt threatened to derail the contract so Governor William D. Bloxham visited Disston in Philadelphia to persuade him to relieve the debt. During the visit, Disston tentatively agreed to purchase four million acres of Internal Improvement Fund land for 25 cents per acre, an agreement which became a formal contract on June 1, 1881. This made him the largest landowner in the United States. On December 17, 1881, Disston sold two million acres of his land to an English member of Parliament for $600,000. Disston lost most of his fortune as a result of the 1893 financial panic. He committed suicide in 1896.[6] (4.1)

4.1 Portrait of Philadelphia financier Hamilton Disston, Florida Department of State

By reclaiming swamp land by canals and drainage, the Florida frontier in bankruptcy, had plenty of cheap land for agriculture. What it didn't have, but designated in the Land Trust, was railroad infrastructure that would bring the fruits of labor quickly to markets in the north. Railroads as well, brought promise of a new life and fortunes and years of competing interest and bloodshed. Without the railroads, there would have been no mining boom, and definitely no land boom. After Hamilton Disston, two more northerners would make their fortunes and bring about the Florida that we know today; railroad barons Henry Flagler and Henry Plant.

Connecticut born Henry B. Plant (4.2) came to Florida to take care of his wife's health needs. Much like Disston, who came to fish, Plant's visits resulted in huge gains. He grew fond of Southern ways. After the Civil War, Plant believed that the South would rebound economically, but the key to that recovery would be transportation systems. With funds made during the war, Plant began buying up destitute Southern railroads and building new ones. His Plant System began, ironically, in the lowlands around Charleston, South Carolina. In 1882, Plant's investment company purchased the bankrupted Georgia railroad system, the Savannah, Florida and Western Railroad, which became

4.2 Portrait of Henry B. Plant, Florida Department of State

the Plant System. Plant could have never seen what his choices in 1882 would end up producing.

Ten years later, Plant was able to purchase the defunct Florida Southern Railroad. This extensive East-West, North -South rail line gave birth to an economically viable Florida with tourism, agriculture and mining. Between 1884 and 1886, the Southern line reached Plant City and the Great Tampa Bay. By 1886, his rails reached Punta Gorda, and then the end of the line on Charlotte Harbor in that same year (4.3). The progress achieved was truly remarkable.[7] By 1888, people could travel by rail between New York City and the New South, all the way to Tampa, Florida, no small accomplishment.

By 1890, it was the railroad that brought all of the speculators and investors, and starting in the 1890's, railroads brought tourists and winter vacationers for the new resorts and hotels built by the railroad magnets.(4.4) (4.5) An ad by Plant's Charlotte Harbor & Northern railroad, which ran in Florida's newspapers in the late 1800s, repeats what the earlier white settlers promoted before and after the Civil War. The ad went so far as to hold a contest to "win a home where lands are cheap and returns from them are certain." The ad claimed something the earlier farmers knew to be false, namely the lands below Arcadia were free of frost. The entire ad continued the narrative that Florida from Charlotte Harbor south was a tropical agricultural paradise (4.6). Agricultural speculators took up the call and many of them in the next several decades lost their shirts. Even as early as 1881, settlers in the Southern regions of the River lauded the resources for living and growing fruit in the region. A most curious ad was placed that mixed lemons with phosphate as the reason to jump aboard the new railroad to speculate on the land there, and specifically using phosphate fields as a major drawing card.(4.7)

The railroads also brought the first archaeologists in search of treasures and lost civilizations. The Smithsonian launched the famous Pepper-Hearst Expedition of 1895–1896 led by Frank Hamilton Cushing.[8] He was soon followed by self-endowed Philadelphia pot hunter Clarence B. Moore. The early archaeologists could now explore southern Florida due to Plant's rail connections from the Port at Jacksonville.

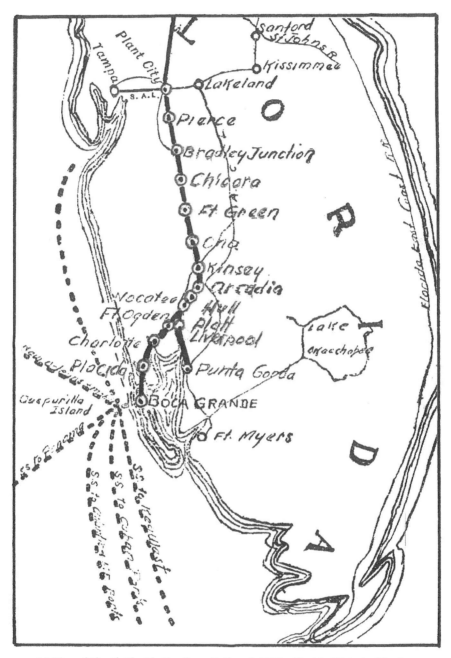

4.3 Map of Plant's Florida Southern Railroad, 1890s. Florida Historical Society

4.4 Rail Depot at Boca Grande, Charlotte Harbor, Florida Department of State

4.5 Hotel Punta Gorda 1910, Florida Department of State

4.7 Florida Southern Railroad land contest Advertisement, Florida Department of State

Wanted, Five Thousand Farmers and Gardeners!

From Ohio, Indiana, Illinois, Michigan and Iowa to go on our

HOME ✸ SEEKERS' ✸ EXCURSION
──── TO ────

FLORIDA!

──── VIA THE NEW LINE OF THE ────

Florida Central and Peninsular Railroad,

The Shortest, Quickest and Best Route to Florida.

✸ NOVEMBER 6 AND DECEMBER 4, 1894. ✸

Half ✸ Fare ✸ for ✸ Round ✸ Trip.

Don't fail to visit Charlotte Harbor, Florida, the greatest commercial sea-port, health and pleasure resort of the South, where may be seen steamships loading for home and foreign ports with Phosphate and other products. This harbor embraces the healthiest and richest portion of the State. Here are located the greatest Phosphate fields and market on earth. The home of the Tarpon or Silver-King; the paradise of the sportsman; fish and oysters in untold quantities, and where may be seen growing oranges, grape fruit, lemons, guaves, bananas, mangoes, cocoanuts, dates, citron, strawberries, peaches, plums, pears, apricots, grapes, corn and the finest of tobacco and pine apples. FINE BEACH, HIGH LAND TO WATER'S EDGE. Here your brow is fanned by the gentle breezes of Arcadian mildness, and which brings relief to the invalid and is a positive cure for catarrhal, bronchial and rheumatic troubles. **NO SWAMPS! NO MALARIA! NO LAGRIPPE!** We have for sale valuable fruit, vegetable and phosphate lands, divided into tracts of 10 acres each, in the town of Charlotte Harbor. We have also for sale choice Building Lots, 58x128 feet, in the town of Charlotte Harbor ranging from $10 to $25 per lot. One of these tracts properly cultivated will bring in more income to the owner than any 160 acre farm in Ohio, Indiana or Illinois. Here is the natural home of the PINEAPPLE, where it reaches its greatest perfection in both flavor and size. The Egyptian Queen being one of the finest varieties and which matures here in from 6 to 12 months, from 8,000 to 10,000 plants are put on an acre, and each plant bears from one to five apples weighing from 10 to 15 pounds each, and continues to bear from 6 to 7 years; meanwhile other plants are propagated by slips from the parent stock. A pineapple plantation in this section will net its owner from $500 to $1,500 per acre.

To each Cash Purchaser of ten or more acres of this Land, we will Refund the amount of your fare to Florida.

This proposition holds good for both of these excursions for parties buying land of us. Be sure and call on C. M. DENHAM, or S. J. HEWETT, Charlotte Harbor, Florida, who will show you the lands.

Ask your Ticket Agent for a Ticket to Florida, reading Florida Central and Peninsular R. R., via Columbia, S. C., Savannah, Ga., Everett, Ga., River Junction, Florida, or Lake City, Florida, our five connecting points for Northern Routes for Orlando, Plant City or Tampa, to CHARLOTTE HARBOR, FLORIDA.

See Map, on opposite page, of our new line.

For Rates, Map, and Prices of Florida Lands, call on or address

C. F. McKhann, Cincinnati, Ohio.

NO. 89 JOHNSON BUILDING.

*4.6 Large Florida Southern Railroad Advertisement for Charlotte Harbor 1880s,
Florida Department of State*

61

*4.8 Phosphate laden train leaves Coronet mine in Bone Valley 1920,
Florida Department of State*

Initially the role of the railroads for hauling phosphate was coincidental. But in the case of Marion County, for instance, mining companies laid track and built engines to ensure their product's transport to port. Further south the railroad made the extensive mining in the Bone Valley possible and profitable into the twenty-first century. (4.8)

In Florida after the Civil War, entrepreneurs were laying rails that began in the North, bringing people and goods from the only established port city, Jacksonville, to both coasts. Initially these early Florida railroads grew predictably in reasonable course. After all, land and earlier railroads were bought in foreclosure. The discovery of phosphate, however, accelerated both the need and speed of connecting rails, with mining companies financing tracks and engines in the interior and Gulf coastal regions. Mined phosphates in the north, like those mined in Live Oaks (4.9), needed rail to transport processed phosphate to Jacksonville. Those mines on the Peace River in Bone Valley needed to be transported down river to Charlotte Harbor.

4.9 *Live Oaks Rail Depot at Port Inglis, Citrus County, Florida Department of State*

4.10 *Phosphate barge on Peace River, Florida Department of State*

(4.10) The history clearly shows that the railroads preceded the discovery of phosphates in Florida. But as luck would have it, those betting heavily on Florida phosphates and setting up mining companies, had the necessary connecting lines exactly when they needed them. Railroads brought towns, merchants, physicians, school teachers and lawyers to support mining, cattle, lumber and citrus growing. After the turn-of-the-century, and as competition increased, Florida phosphate companies could no longer afford to use railroads to transport the phosphates to ports. The history of the Florida mining boom and bust, and others like it, is a history of changing fortunes. In 2018, almost everyone has heard of Tampa Bay, but few have heard of Charlotte Harbor in Florida.

By coincidence, two people named Henry brought railroads to the Florida frontier. The other, Henry Flagler, received contracts and built railroads, hotels and towns from Jacksonville all the way to Key West. Flagler had little effect on phosphate mining, but I bring up his efforts for his business practices. Flagler's railroad empire, unlike Plant's, was built on convict labor. Most Americans know of the railroads using Chinese laborers to build the first transcontinental railroads. Few know, however, that many freed blacks left Florida after the Civil War, leaving the roads and railroads to be built by convicts. Southern business interests, all too accustomed to the institution of slavery, found themselves short of labor. The earliest mining companies, such as Live Oak and Dunnellon, relied on a system using convicts (4.11), who were African-American, to be their miners. Flagler, it turns out, maximized personal profits by not having to pay a decent wage for a day's work. All parts of the Bone Valley handled the new industrialization and the changes it brought differently. In the Southern region around Charlotte Harbor, for instance, phosphate mining companies did not use convict labor, but turpentine manufacturers certainly did. (4.12) From 1900 to 1910 more single men worked in turpentine mills than in fishing or mining. South near Punta Gorda was a large distillery. A study of Punta Gorda's 1900 U.S. Census clearly shows most young single men worked in the new turpentine industry.[9] Florida was a large turpentine processing company which employed white workers. A little north of there, in Southland and in Sarasota County, were other turpentine processing companies that only used black convict labor.[10] I found a U.S. Census that actually listed all the convicts. Such[11] were the choices. From my research it appears that it most likely had to be a moral choice, or a practical choice (paid labor worked harder than forced labor, or both). That is what I refer to as the gray areas. The new industries, capitalism and the market, ended up changing views and behavior, once considered in terms of black or white. I discovered that Florida had very little to do with Yankee v Southern sensibilities. Some of the more discriminatory views toward blacks were by Floridians whose roots were in the

4.11 Florida convict laborers, Florida Department of State

4.12 Convict turpentine laborers, Florida Department of State

north. Case in point, Henry Flagler was the son of a New York state Presbyterian minister.

In a May 17,2018 article written by Bryan Bowman and Kathy Roberts Forde in the *Washington Post*, entitled "How slave labor built the state of Florida — decades after the Civil War," they state what few Americans know,

> that Flagler built his tourist empire — and modern Florida — by exploiting two brutal labor systems that blanketed the South for 50 years after the Civil War: convict leasing and debt peonage. Created to preserve the white supremacist racial order and to address the South's labor shortages, these systems targeted African Americans, stealing their labor and entrapping them in state-sanctioned forms of involuntary servitude.[12]

As a writer of what I refer to as Forgotten Florida, there are those parts of Florida's history that simply got lost over time. But the chapter about the convict labor system is one Florida wants very much to disappear. The person leading the deletion from the history books was Flagler himself. Bowman and Forde further state:

> When the U.S. Justice Department, African American leaders and northern muckraking journalists exposed Flagler's labor practices, he colluded with powerful government, newspaper and business interests in Florida to whitewash public knowledge and, by extension, the historical record itself. Committed to preserving his and the state's reputation, Flagler co-opted powerful news outlets to spread distorted versions of events.[13]

Throughout the South, convict lease laws criminalized blackness, providing a means for authorities to arrest freed people for made up-crimes such as vagrancy, lease them to private companies and force their labor. For Florida, convict leasing generated revenue and provided a tool to intimidate and control black citizens. For private businesses, the state offered vulnerable laborers who could be worked beyond human endurance and brutalized at a whim.

Henry Flagler was more famous as the partner of John D. Rockefeller in the founding of the Standard Oil Company. But to many he represents the greed and exploitation of America's industrialists during the Gilded Age. In the context of this book, he provides an important contrast to his railroad contemporary in Florida, Henry Plant. Plant's Florida Southern line brought Northern industrialist Cornelius Vanderbilt to the end of the line, where he built the large and luxurious Hotel Punta Gorda overlooking Charlotte Harbor in the late 1880's. Again, a study in contrasts, the future of Florida for a brief time coexisted with a wild frontier Florida.

Today, all of the train depots and stations remain sans the tracks of the Plant System Railroad in Florida. The rail-bridge built across the water used to transport phosphate to the shipping port at Boca Grande stands in pieces. All are reminders of Florida's early days mining the gray gold. (4.13)

The removal of many Plant System and Florida Southern Railway System tracks in 1981 appears to be somewhat premature. By the twenty-first century, due to fuel prices, vessel, barge and truck transport of phosphate product cost more than rail transport.

4.13 Remains of phosphate railroad bridge to Boca Grande,
Courtesy of gassparillaislandlifestyle.com

Florida phosphate giant Mosaic, on their sustainability website, reported that in 2015, the company shipped 67.4% of their in process and finished goods by rail, approximately 45 million tons.

Nowhere in the history of Florida are the dramatic changes that were the shift from an agrarian way of life to industrialization found than in the Florida Gulf shipping ports. Prior to the Civil War, the few ports that had yet to be deepened were busy in Cuban-American trade in both cattle and produce. Ports competed for dominance. In the case of the Great Tampa Bay, two neighboring ports, Tampa and Hillsborough, were in constant intensive competition.

Shifting fortunes, characterized Florida towns and port cities after the Civil War. Cedar Key was one of the more populated centers with about 10,000 people. During the pioneer days, goods came down the Mississippi and transported on the Gulf to Cedar Key. Early rail service then took them to cities in the northeast; therefore, Cedar Key prospered as the middleman. Later, commodities such as cedar, produce and seafood produced locally, made Cedar Key a major exporting port. Oysters left the deep-water port there for ports all over the southeast. In the day, steamships routinely traveled with goods between New Orleans, Cedar Key and Havana.

Henry Plant made his mark by purchasing the defaulted Southern rail lines. He believed he had all the lines, but soon discovered that he had not purchased the railhead at Cedar Key. The owners refused to sell Cedar Key to Plant. This forced Plant to abandon his plans and move his line to the then small village of Tampa (4.14), but not till he started steamer service from the island. The rest, as they say is history. The rebuke of Plant's railroad and a devastating hurricane of 1896 resulted in the population leaving; Cedar Key, and not Tampa, became a small fishing village.[14]

During the Civil War and post war years, shipping and commerce on the sea was interrupted. Pioneer Florida during the 1800's had the major Atlantic port at Jacksonville. For commerce, Florida also relied on Cedar Key on the Gulf Coast and Key West, the most important commercial port for goods and commerce. Prior to the railroads and phosphate mining, plantation owners, citrus growers and cattlemen had to get their goods to one of the

4.14 Plants Steamer leaving Cedar Key, Florida Department of State

ports. Port Tampa, Port Inglis and Boca Grande and Punta Rasa. The largest ships to visit and dock were sailing schooners (4.15).

Port Inglis was the first to benefit greatly as a phosphate shipping port for the rail cars and barges of the mined phosphate coming out of the early Dunnellon area mines. Soon however, rail became the most economical way of getting the rock to the Atlantic seaports.

With mining, came the need for freighters, many freighters, and that meant deep waters. Anyone who frequents the Florida Gulf coast knows that shallow waters define the Gulf Coast. Even the native people learned early in the European conquest of the peninsula, the difficulty large vessels encountered. The bounty of precious metals from shipwrecks in and around the Florida Keys, made many of the local chiefs wealthy over time.

No other Florida town reflects the dramatic boom and bust of the once phosphate capital of the world then Boca Grande. Boca Grande, the little village on the southern tip of Gasparilla Island in Lee County, sits on the only pass into Charlotte Harbor and the Peace River deep enough for the phosphate laden barges to unload their product onto ocean-going freighters for export (4.16). In the 1800's and 1900's, the port at Boca Grande, competed with the Ports at Tampa and Hillsborough in the north and Punta Rasa

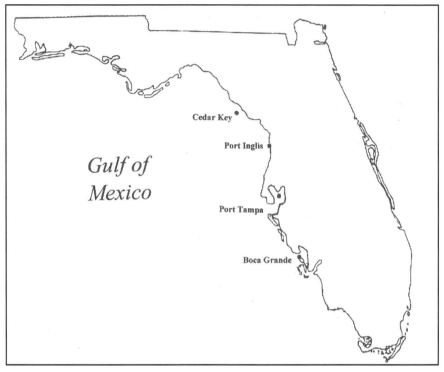

4.15 Map of Gulf ports, Ted Ehmann

4.16 Aerial view of phosphate bins and docks at Boca Grande, Florida Department of State

4.17 Plant's Tampa Bay Hotel under construction 1880s, Florida Department of State

in the south. With all the ports on the extensive Gulf Coast of the Florida peninsula, only these four were deep enough to handle the large shipping vessels that were needed to move the processed phosphate to fertilizer companies on the East Coast and in Europe.

While the phosphate boom brought together strange bedfellows, it also advanced the railroad interests. The railroads which started as passenger lines, soon transported thousands of dollars' worth of phosphate to the port towns. The landscapes of the Gulf ports were transformed overnight with towering phosphate bins and towers, cranes and loading docks.

Plant's Plant System intended to bring wintering vacationers to his luxurious waterfront hotel (4.17) on Tampa Bay. It ended up transforming the small fishing port (4.18) into a major city and industrial port due to the increased phosphate mining in nearby Bone Valley. Likewise, the transformation of the fishing village of Tampa to a major world port is still ongoing with an impressive history. A group of prominent citizens pooled their funds and bought up much of the waterfront immediately after the war. Their success and investment resulted in Henry Plant's decision to take his Florida Southern Railroad to Old Port Tampa. Soon Old Port

4.18 Bird's eye view of Tampa 1870-1889,
Florida Department of State

Tampa was connected to New York City, a reality thought to be impossible only a few years earlier (4.19).

By 1898, the Port of Tampa prospered with phosphates and Cuban cigars, but then war came once more. Cuba's war of independence was followed by the Spanish-American War. In May of 1898, then Lt. Col. Theodore Roosevelt, hundreds of Rough Riders and their horses arrived at the port. The Port of Tampa became important to the war effort. Unknown to the United States and the world, Tampa's strategic role in the attack on Cuba made the port famous, without its traffic of phosphate- laden ships headed for world ports.

Important to Florida in the twentieth and twenty-first centuries, Plant's railroad helped to turn Tampa into a deep-water center for freighters and steamers from Cuba and South America. The rail line opened up the region to citrus and vegetable growers, for it no longer took twenty days to reach Northern markets by boat. Soon

4.19 Rail Depot at Tampa Port, Florida Department of State

to follow were investors for trolley lines and electric companies. Plant built the largest of his hotels on the Hillsborough River. The Tampa Bay Hotel charged $100 a day, attracting the Northern rich.

At the end if the nineteenth century, local business leaders made a concerted effort to enlist the help of the federal government to deepen Tampa harbor's channels. In 1905 Congress was convinced and authorized the U.S. Army Corps of Engineers to dredge to a 20-foot depth. This was the first of four projects to dredge Tampa into a modern, first-class port.

Soon after, legislation allowed for a deepening of the channel to 24 feet, configure new wharfs, build a belt line railroad, and create a Tampa Port Commission. By 1927, a 34 foot channel was approved. The final improvements were authorized in 1970 and work to create a 43-foot-deep main ship channel was begun.

True, many forces came together over time to make Tampa the thriving modern port and city that it is today, but it was phosphate mining that did the lion's share of the work. While today, giant

4.20 Rough Riders, Port of Tampa 1898. Florida Department of State

4.21 Ship leaving for Cuba from Tampa, Spanish-American War, 1898.
Florida Department of State

*4.22 Ship towing phosphate schooner into port at Tampa 1890s,
Florida Department of State*

cruise ships go in and out of Port Tampa, underscoring Florida's largest and most important tourism industry, in an article in *Crop Life,* June 19, 2013, Matt Hopkins quoted the Tampa Port Director on how just important the phosphate mining accounts for the port's prominence:

> Phosphate, a Port of Tampa mainstay export for the past century, accounts for more than two-thirds of the Port's $15.1 billion annual economic activity. In addition, the phosphate industry supports more than half of the Port's 80,000 direct, indirect and related jobs, according to a new study released yesterday by the Tampa Port Authority.[15]

Presently, Mosaic created more than half of the 10,573 direct jobs at the port from the movement of phosphate rock and raw materials, as well as crop nutrition and animal feed supplies and products. Other phosphate-related companies also support this economic activity.

The Port of Tampa connects central Florida, the state's epicenter for phosphate mining and production, to consumers both domestically and internationally. The regional phosphate fertilizer industry accounts for nearly 12 million tons, or roughly 35 percent, of cargo through the Port of Tampa. *BaySoundings.com* recently highlighted the port's accomplishments from the benefits derived from Florida phosphate:

> That pride is not without justification. In Hillsborough County, the phosphate industry and related shipping concerns pump billions of dollars into the local economy. Phosphate-related products are the #1 export out of the Port of Tampa, and fuel U.S. dominance in world trade of ammonium phosphate. By providing American farmers with 75% of their fertilizer needs, Florida phosphate is a chief reason why food prices in this country remain relatively low, for now.[16]

Even with Mosaic announcing in 2018 that it will be moving its world headquarters to Tampa Bay, the company's recent closings and downsizing, along with their investments in Saudi Arabia, mean that this will be the last hurrah. Since the USGS reports at the end of the twentieth century, Florida's deposits have peaked. The port of Tampa will more than likely lose its Gulf of Mexico phosphate shipping business to the Persian Gulf.

ENDNOTES

[1] floridahistory.org/railroads.htm

[2] *Ibid.*

[3] https://en.wikipedia.org/wiki/Hamilton_Disston

[4] *Ibid.*

[5] myfloridahistory.org/.../armed-occupation-act

[6] https://en.wikipedia.org/wiki/Hamilton_Disston

[7] https://en.wikipedia.org/wiki/Henry_B._Plant

[8] https://en.wikipedia.org/wiki/Pepper–Hearst_expedition

[9] 1900 U.S. Census, DeSoto County, FL

[10] 1900 U.S. Census, Manatee County, FL

[11] *Ibid.*

[12] Bryan Bowman and Kathy Roberts Forde, *Washington Times*, May 17, 2018

[13] *Ibid.*

[14] en.wikipedia.org/wiki/1896_Cedar_Keys_hurricane

[15] *www.croplife.com/crop-inputs/fertilizer/.*

[16] baysoundings.com/legacy-archives/sum05/phosphate6.html

THE MINING BOOM
YEARS IN BONE VALLEY

American history is full of stories of precious mineral reserve discoveries in the West. This is the first book to tell the story of the discovery of a less-known mineral in great demand in the Deep South. The phosphate mining boom was the first opportunity to industrialize presented to the people and communities in the South following the Civil War. As such, it is appropriate to view it in the context of a possible economic comeback. Beginning in the Lowlands of South Carolina and Charleston, communities devasted by the war, phosphate for fertilizer created new economic opportunities to the wealthy and the poor alike. One of original colonies, South Carolina was anything but unsettled. Florida was a different matter entirely.

Very recently settled, Florida was depleted of its already small and struggling population by the war's end. The state was in deep debt. The only thing Florida had was land, plenty of unsettled land, of which the majority was under water. As such, there was no infrastructure: roads, bridges and railroads. Its labor force had fled and carpetbaggers had descended to administer its new order, a new order from no order. Florida was always about outsiders and outsiders were always interested in Florida, until they came up empty handed. The only exceptions being those who fled domination and/or capture in the neighboring United States. Unsettled Florida, therefore was, and to a great extent has been, about new money and not more money from old money. Somehow, these speculators are motivated by the supply of large amounts of cheap land. The mining boom in Florida's Bone Valley falls entirely into this short, but predictable history.

Prior to the Civil War, much of the wealth in Florida was concentrated in the central interior of the state. There the environment and its few inhabitants matched as closely as possible, the large cotton-producing plantations of its neighbors in the Deep South. However, by the war's end, plantations, farms and homesteads had been systematically burned and looted by Yankee troops. The entire Bone Valley had become radically depopulated.[1] Devastated by the war, Polk and Manatee Counties became a new battleground during Reconstruction. Waves of new immigrants flooded the Peace River Valley and settled there, controlling the vote and the political future of the frontier. The Republicans were clearly in the ascendance in Polk County, while in neighboring Manatee County the Democrats, known as the 'conservatives,' had control.[2] During this period of time, Manatee County included today's Hardee, DeSoto, Charlotte, Highlands, Glades and Sarasota Counties. Important to the phosphate mining history, the phosphate rich deposits lie in Manatee, DeSoto, Hardee and parts of Charlotte County, as well as neighboring Polk County. In 1870, the entire population of the immense Manatee County was only 1,931[3] with few blacks remaining. Two-thirds of the population of Manatee County lived along the Peace River Valley. During Reconstruction waves of immigrants, refugees from other states, soon redrew the political landscape and outnumbered the Republicans. It is important to state that one group of settlers in the Peace River Valley came back virtually untouched by the war, the cattlemen. They owned their properties and held power and influence in the valley. Cattlemen were the only ones to have grown wealthier during the war. These primarily Confederate cattlemen, who all fought to rid the area of the Seminole and then formed cow calvaries to protect shipments of cattle to the Confederate forces, lost very little. By the war's end, due to a lucrative cattle trade with Havana, they became gold-rich, and those that invested in their efforts prospered as well. Cheap land for grazing cattle became golden soon after the war. Cheap land with phosphate reserves would soon rival their golden calves. A study of the market prices for heads of cattle vs. tons of phosphate in the 1890s provides a picture of what will happen in Bone Valley in the twentieth century and beyond. Speaking of pictures, the history of the mining boom

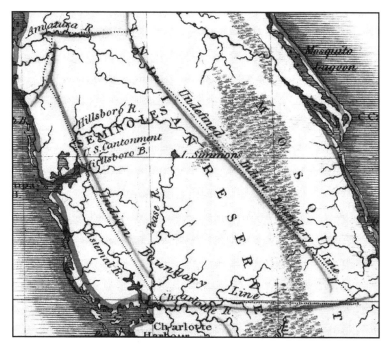

5.1 Map showing Indian Reserved Lands central Florida 1850s,
Courtesy of South Florida University

in the Bone Valley is filled with photographs which document the unique mining culture that took hold there and which continues to shape the region's future, for better or for worse.

Immediately after the war, the new immigrants were dirt poor farmers. Squatters who took over the lands taken from the Indians decades earlier, as you can see in this 1850's map showing the area as Indian Reserved (5.1). Their farming citrus growing predecessors were ruined by the war since they lost their labor force via emancipation. The new farmers changed the physical and human landscape of the Peace River Valley. Unlike where they came from, Bone Valley was everything, a frontier and wilderness. It had few or no schools, churches, transportation, towns or stores. The fertile lands, while plentiful, were isolated, having no railroads, telegraphs, or regular mail delivery. The new farmers soon discovered that extreme weather events in the area were commonplace and their fortunes were constantly threatened by wind, rain and frost. In 1878 and 1879 nature lashed out, playing

5.2 Florida settlers 1900, Florida Department of State

total havoc on their new lives and industry. Even with the influx of refugees immigrating to settle and farm the vast acreage along the Peace River in Manatee County, the population by the early 1880's was only 3,505 people,[4] mostly poor white farmers (5.2).

You might assume, based on the outcomes of landowners during speculation in other mining booms in American history, all benefited greatly from the skyrocketing land prices. Historian Canter Brown, Jr. revealed through his research that decisions by the Florida Legislature made it so these new settlers in Bone Valley, unlike the western territories, did not and could not own their lands.[5] Therefore, at the very beginning of phosphate speculation in the late 1880's, those interested in land purchases for mining along the Peace River found few lands had clear property titles. Prior to the war, the state put the lands along the Peace River in a trust.

The Swamp and Overflowed Lands Act of 1850 transferred millions of acres to the state for drainage and reclamation.[6] Not an issue at the time, but when phosphate pebbles in the river and adjoining lands were discovered thirty years later, such restrictions became troublesome. Those lands not within the trust could be purchased for twenty-five cents on the dollar,[7] but the new immigrants who now lived and worked those lands as homesteaders lacked even those resources by which to purchase their property.

In 1881, the same year that LeBaron surveyed the Peace River Valley for a possible canal project, desperate for funds, the State of Florida and then Governor William D. Bloxham made an agreement with Philadelphia businessman, Hamilton Disston. Florida sold four million acres of land for a million dollars. Disston's Florida Land and Development Company now owned 102,000 acres in Polk County and 370,000 acres in Manatee County. Squatters in Bone Valley were given two years to purchase their claims now from the developer for $1.25 an acre.[8]

After 1881, increase in demand for farmland along the Peace River, by newly arrived homesteaders from Georgia, Alabama, Tennessee and North Carolina became consistent. Bone Valley was being repopulated by white farmers. No one could have predicted the intense changes about to occur. Before 1887 and the discovery of phosphate, acreage in the Bone Valley for farming and cattle raising could be purchased for $1.25 to $1.50 an acre. In the next few years, land close to the river jumped to $25.00, then $50.00 and even $300.00 an acre.[9] New mining towns like Phosphoria, Pebbledale and Acme in Polk County reflected the new transformation driven entirely by northern and European speculators. *The Arcadian Newspaper* around March of 1890 announced:

> The Peace River phosphate beds excite the wonder of all who see them. And fertilizer men pronounce them the finest in the world. The day is not far off when phosphate works will line the banks of the Peace River from Bowling Green south. Thousands of hands will be employed and much capital will be invested. DeSoto County is destined to be the richest county in Florida.[10]

Such predictions did come to be true, except for DeSoto County's wealth. In fact, the following year, cotton prices fell and with that so did demand for fertilizers. The smaller companies, even before the Panic of 1893, went bankrupt.

The boom in river pebble phosphate mining in Florida was made possible because unlike South Carolina, the State of Florida did not jump in to regulate river mining. If you had the capital, you could invest. I was surprised to read in Brown's book that several local residents pooled their resources and formed mining companies. Moore and Tantum set up a company near Homeland, other residents set up the Homeland Phosphate and Fertilizer Company. Judge T.W. Anderson was part of the Whitaker Phosphate and Fertilizer Company. J.E. Robeson of Fort Meade and Isaac Whitaker of Homeland were both principals in the new Fort Meade Phosphate, Fertilizer, Land and Improvement Company in Polk County.[11]

The labor-intensive river pebble mining production along the Peace River increased to 56,000 ton in 1890.[12] (5.3) By 1892, the valley had eighteen different companies producing over 354, 000 tons of phosphate. Unlike South Carolina's lowlands, fertilizer industries were not generated as a result of the intense mining operations. In 1890, the one and only fertilizer plant opened at Fort Meade.[13] All of this phosphate production was achieved using migrant black labor.[14]

It is impossible to get an accurate picture of the number of people involved in mining operations during the boom phase in Bone Valley. For instance, federal census records in and in DeSoto County during those peak years. When the boom went bust by the early 1900's the "new" mining towns were never visited or recorded. This is why I conclude that the early phosphate mining boom was executed using transient and imported labor who lived in make-shift

Year	Long tons	Year	Long tons	Year	Long tons
1888	3, 000	1896	100, 052	1904	81, 030
1889	8, 100	1897	97, 763	1905	87, 847
1890	46. 501	1898	79, 000	1906	41, 463
1891	54, 500	1899	88, 953	1907	36, 185
1892	f102, 820	1900	59, 863	1908 [2]	11, 160
1893	122, 820	1901	46, 974		
1894	102, 307	1902	5, 055	Total	1, 305, 007
1895	73, 036	1903	56, 578		

Production of Florida river-pebble phosphate 1888-1908

[1] Includes 12,120 tons carried over from preceding year.
[2] Some rock sold during 1911-14, but figures not reported separately; probably hold-over material, as it is stated elsewhere that none was produced after 1908.

5.3 Chart showing tonnage, Peace River phosphates. Florida Department of State

5.4 Young miners, DeSoto County, 1890s, Florida Department of State
Fort Meade Historical Society

housing or tents. (5.4) Of the previously settled towns along the
Peace River, none of the residents between 1890 and the 1900
census were involved in phosphate mining or operations. There is
one exception, the town of Fort Ogden. Fort Ogden in only a few
decades was an example of the bust that followed the boom. By
1910, not a single cattleman remained. By 1910, the black families
had all left with the end of the river phosphate industry. So too had
the farmers. The entire community besides merchants, doctors
and railroad employees were orange growers. Further down river
Punta Gorda, now surpassed Fort Ogden in population. The census
reveals the cattle industry had left and most men worked in the new
turpentine industry or fishing. The phosphate port, down harbor
at Boca Grande, remained as a phosphate shipping port into the
1960's. The March 1890 pronouncement in the DeSoto County
newspaper, *The Arcadian*, about DeSoto County becoming the
wealthiest county in the state was pure fantasy. The inhabitants in
the DeSoto County portion of Bone Valley came and went, and have
come and gone for decades since.

5.5 Main Street, Fort Mead 1890, Florida Department of State

5.6 Fort Meade School House, Florida Department of State

5.7 Fort Meade Baseball Team, 1910, Florida Department of State

5.8 Fort Meade band, 1910, Florida Department of State

5.9 Tent revival meeting, Bone Valley, 1890s, Florida Department of State

Fort Meade, which began as a critical safety harbor for the new settlers during the second Seminole War, was totally transformed by the ever-increasing mining there. Once a fort with a few growers and cattle families, it soon built up to accommodate the steady flow of mine workers. The short tree-lined Main Street (5.5) boomed between 1890 and 1910 thanks to the new prospects, the phosphate boom, and the new railroad. A hotel, a saloon, a bank and finally a large school were constructed.(5.6). Recreation became available for the first time in the once wilderness community. There was a racetrack, a baseball team (5.7), and even a town band to play for special occasions (5.8). A new Episcopal church was built and tent revival meetings (5.9) filed their Sundays. Young people would gather on the banks of the Peace River (5.10), and at least for a while, there was a very settled life in the towns between the mining fields.

*5.10 Young people picnic on the banks of the Peace River, Bartow,
Florida Department of State*

With dramatically shifting demographics driven by the phosphate mining fever in the Bone Valley, a small outpost located at the headwaters of the Peace River was renamed after an early officer casualty of the Civil War. Bartow would become the county seat of Polk County. Polk County would become the phosphate capital of Florida. Initially, its roots were in cattle ranching, and it was the wealthy cattle king, Joseph Summerlin (5.11) who donated the large tract of land for the building of the new courthouse. Large and impressive, the very ornate building is more like a state capitol, especially when viewing the central rotunda from inside. When the phosphate was discovered, the town of Bartow in the interior highlands had only 4,000 residents. After 1880, it mushroomed in population and size, as the grand courthouse shows, to become the fifteenth most-populous city in Florida.[15] In the first few decades

*5.11 Jacob Summerlin,
Florida Department of State*

LAKELAND EVENING TELEGRAM, SATURDAY, MAY 14, 1921   PAGE TWO

Polk County's Phosphate Industry

Output of Mines Increased Over 100 Per Cent. in Year 1920 With Bright Future Ahead of Industry Which Brings Millions To This Favored Region

FLORIDA produces 82 per cent of the phosphate mined in the United States. Its total yield for the year 1920, which exceeded all former years, was 3,369,384 tons, which sold at an average price of $5.78 a ton, the total amount received thus falling but little short of $20,000,000. Of this, Polk County produced fully 70 per cent.

It has the largest phosphate deposits in the world. The list of mining companies at the end of this article gives some idea of the extent of the business which is yet in its infancy, since the public is just learning to depend upon Florida phosphate as the basis of their commercial fertilizers, and the demand for it is being marvellously stimulated by the increasing prosperity of the South.

The following extracts from a bulletin issued by Herman Gunter, State Geologist, give an adequate idea of the magnitude of this business:

"The phosphate industry of Florida in 1920 far exceeded that of any previous year, both in point of production and of value. This fact is brought out by statistics collected in co-operation with the United States Geological Survey and recently tabulated. The total shipment of phosphate from Florida during 1920 was 3,369,384 long tons, as compared with 1,660,200 long tons in 1919. This is an increase of 1,709,184 tons, which is more than twice the production for the previous year. The year 1913 is referred to as the "peak" year of the phosphate industry of the State, production that year amounting to 2,545,276 long tons, with a valuation of $9,563,084. It is thus seen the output record for 1920 exceeds the former one by 824,108 tons and in value by $9,901,278. The quantity of phosphate rock mined and marketed during 1920 from the whole United States was 4,103,982 long tons. Of this amount, from the figures above given, it will be seen that Florida produced 82 per cent.

The following table gives the production and value of the three varieties of phosphate rock produced in Florida for the years 1919 and 1920:

1919

Variety	Quantity (Long Tons)	Value	Average Value Per Ton
Hard Rock	265,467	$2,425,563	$ 8.59
Soft Rock	14,498	196,318	13.54
Land Pebble	1,500,235	5,149,048	3.70
	1,660,200	$7,797,929	$ 4.70

1920

Variety	Quantity (Long Tons)	Value	Average Value Per Ton
Hard Rock	403,249	$4,525,191	$11.31
Soft Rock	13,953	109,551	13.66
Land Pebble	2,955,182	14,748,620	4.99
	3,369,384	$19,464,362	$ 5.78

The recovery of the industry from the depressing conditions attributable to the recent world war is shown both in the largely increased production from the pebble phosphate fields and the very decided increase from the hard rock fields, as compared with the output for several preceding years. The amount of hard rock phosphate marketed during 1920 is evidence of the increased demand for this high grade rock. Soft phosphate maintained the record set in 1919, practically the same quantity being marketed in 1920 as in that year.

The most striking increase in production for the year was from the pebble phosphate field, where the amount marketed total 1,594,947 tons more than in 1919. The average value per ton for the pebble rock increased from $3.79 in 1919 to $4.99 in 1920. The hard rock production increased 114,782 tons. The average value of this variety increased from $8.59 per ton in 1919 to $11.31 in 1920. For soft phosphate there was

a slight decrease in the amount marketed, the average value per ton remaining practically the same in 1920 as in 1919.

The total production of phosphate rock in Florida since the beginning of the industry in 1888 to the close of 1920, according to statistics collected by the Florida Geological Survey and the United States Geological Survey, is estimated to be 40,239,898 tons, with a total valuation of $156,318,078.

LIST OF PHOSPHATE MINING COMPANIES OPERATING IN POLK COUNTY

American Agricultural Chemical Co., 2 Rector St., New York, N. Y., and Pierce, Fla.

American Cyanamid Co., 511 Fifth Ave., New York, N. Y., and Brewster, Fla.

Armour Fertilizer Works, 209 W. Jackson Blvd., Chicago, Ill., and Bartow, Fla.

Charleston, S. C., Mining & Manufacturing Co., Richmond, Va., and Ft. Meade, Fla.

Florida Phosphate Mining Corporation, P. O. Box 1118, Norfolk, Va., and Bartow, Fla.

Independent Chemical Co., 33 Pine St., New York, N. Y., and Mulberry.

International Agricultural Corporation, 61 Broadway, New York, N. Y., and Mulberry, Fla.

Morris Fertilizer Co., 801 Citizens & Southern Bank Bldg., Atlanta, Ga., and Pierce, Fla.

Palmetto Phosphate Co., 2 Rector St., New York, N. Y., and Tiger Bay, Fla.

Phosphate Mining Co., 55 John St., New York, N. Y., and Nichols, Fla.

L. N. Pipkin, Mulberry, Fla.

Societe Universelles de Mines, Industrie, Commerce et Agriculture, Pembroke, Fla.

Southern Phosphate Corporation, 25 Broad St., New York, N. Y., and Lakeland, Fla.

Swift & Co., Union Stock Yards, Chicago, Ill., and Bartow, Fla.

ADDITIONAL INFORMATION

For detailed information and illustrated folders write to the Publicity Department Polk County Board of County Commissioners at Bartow, the Fort Meade Chamber of Commerce, the Frost Proof Board of Trade, the Lake Wales Board of Trade, the Lake Hamilton Board of Trade, the Haines City Board of Trade, the Lake Alfred Board of Trade, the Auburndale Chamber of Commerce, the Winter Haven Board of Trade, the Lakeland Chamber of Commerce, or the Bartow Board of Trade.

THIS PUBLICITY HAS BEEN MADE POSSIBLE BY THE COOPERATION OF

5.12 Advertisement Lakeland Evening Telegraph 1921. National Archives

of the twentieth-century, thousands of acres of land around the city were strip mines. Overnight, Bartow was the hub for the largest phosphate industry in the United States. Unlike their antebellum predecessors, the mansions in Bartow were built by the sweat of miners from near and far.

The 1920s in Florida was a growth time for the state as a whole. The coastal areas experienced an unbelievable land boom. In the interior, the mining towns and cities in the Bone Valley showed no signs of slowing down. The headline in a full page advertisement in the *Lakeland Evening Telegram*, May 14, 1921, read: "Output of Mines Increased Over 100 Per Cent. In Year 1920 With Bright Future Ahead of Industry Which Brings Millions To This Favored Region."[16] (5.12) The phosphate mining boom, which began in the Lowlands of South Carolina, for a variety of reasons came to an end and was bust in a decade's time. So, too, out west prior to the boom in the Deep South, deposits of the desired minerals were soon exhausted and mines and towns abandoned. In Polk County the mining boom was still going thirty-years after the discovery of the county's plentiful deposits.

Fourteen mining companies were listed on the advertisement as mining in the county in 1921. Polk County in 1920 was the epicenter of the planet's phosphate deposits. It produced 70% of

5.13 Men waiting for mail outside Fort Meade Post Office, Florida Department of State

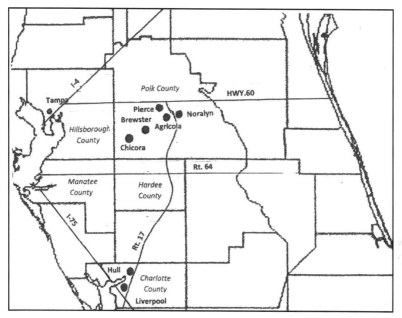

5.14 Map showing location of phosphate mining ghost towns, Ted Ehmann

the 82% of phosphate mined in Florida. At an average price then of $5.78 a ton, it accounted for revenue from mined phosphates of just short of 20 million dollars. This record mining boom was made possible due to the laissez-faire policies of the state. At no time did the government legislate or regulate the mining in the Bone Valley or elsewhere.

The transient quality to life in the Bone Valley at the turn-of-the-century grew into a more stable work force and, there was the ever-growing need for tradesmen, merchants, teachers and doctors. They came from everywhere to the wilderness turned mining country. Fortunately, the railroads filled the transportation needs, but the Peace River valley was still remote, and its newcomers waited every-day for news from home. (5.13)

The market fluctuations routinely forced companies to close mines, and many cases leave Florida and phosphate mining entirely. Except for the county seats of Bartow, and Arcadia in DeSoto County, the mines and towns which boomed during the beginning decades of the twentieth century were abandoned, leaving a trail of ghost towns (5.14) and abandoned mines. The scared landscapes, almost lunar or other-worldly, in many areas still process most of the phosphate for a global market nearby.

The town of Mulberry, the farming community turned mining town, reveals the rapid and total industrialization of life in the Bone Valley by 1910. Other larger company towns like Noralyn and Brewster were abandoned by 1960 and eventually torn down. Others like them disappeared a hundred years ago. Like all cheap land in Florida, real estate developers have an eye on Bone Valley. Since 2012, they have been influencing the Florida legislature to build a highway right through Polk County, one of three new "highway corridors" which will, if completed, transform the Bone Valley and it's people once again.[17]

ENDNOTES

[1] Canter Brown, Jr., 1991, 165-171

[2] *Ibid.*, 221

[3] *Ibid.*, 206

[4] *Ibid.*, 262

[5] *Ibid.*, 258-262

[6] www.llw-law.com/.../Floridas_State_Lands_Authorization.pdf

[7] *Ibid.*

[8] www.llw-law.com/.../Floridas_State_Lands_Authorization.pdf

[9] Canter Brown, Jr., 1991, 315

[10] *The Arcadian*, March 1880

[11] Canter Brown, Jr., 1991, 315

[12] *Ibid.*

[13] *Ibid.*

[14] *Ibid.*

[15] https://en.wikipedia.org/wiki/Bartow,_Florida

[16] *Lakeland Evening Telegram*, May 14, 1921

[17] Gary White, *The Ledger,* May 5, 2019

VI.

A QUICK BUCK: NORTHERN MONEY AND SOUTHERN CHARM

T.D. Allman's realistic search for Florida is filled with comparisons to other pioneer places, such as the great West and its many rich environments that drew different speculators with each discovery of gold and silver, something the limestone peninsula will never be. But even before the dawn of selling Florida resort properties, thousands of speculators got on trains in a rush to secure their fortunes. Allman reminds us of a universal in Florida history: "Because it possesses so few useful resources, the notion that it must be "sold" infests every warp and weave of Florida."[1]

Speculation in phosphate mining in the late 1800's brought together strange bedfellows. Local interests and entrepreneurs could not proceed and be successful in South Carolina, as well as Florida, without large amounts of capital. In order to be competitive one needed to buy as many acres, as many phosphate-producing tracts of land as possible, before the word got out and someone with enough money beat you to the punch. What attracted certain, if not all of the initial speculators and investors in both South Carolina and Florida, was the quick return on investment. Unlike agricultural commodities, phosphate rock was immediately harvestable. Ever-increasing market value, based on demand, guaranteed excellent pricing. All you had to do was secure, extract, clean, crush and transport to a waiting fertilizer company. Compared to gold, it was a gross business measured in tons and not ounces, but nonetheless very profitable.

Joining the mix of monied individuals were the chemists. Often the chemist involved in the discovery and verification of phosphate deposits became investors and even partners. There were the real estate salesmen, all locals with local land knowledge and few ethics. Finally, railroad entrepreneurs who made additional money for their efforts to extend and connect existing rail systems to accommodate the emerging mining concerns. Though the rail lines in Florida were considered and built before phosphate deposits were in the news, railroads played a pivotal role in the boom and subsequent years. Railroad and real estate in Florida were the same ventures by many an industrious individual. The interior of Central Florida, where the phosphates resided, was a remote, vast, and unpopulated area of the state. In short, these deposits, unlike those in South Carolina, were far from ports and cities.

Why the Florida governors and legislators, with all the hype and attention to the phosphate boom, did not insist on a piece of the action is a mystery? Most likely, it was simply that Florida was only a state for forty years before the start of the mining boom, unlike South Carolina which found the first phosphate deposits in the South. Unlike historical Beaufort County and Charleston in South Carolina, the only settlers and interest in the Bone Valley phosphate producing region were farmers. And as such, what infrastructure and basic services that were available in 1886 were those available to growers.

When phosphate rock was first discovered in the Bone Valley, those established businessmen who had property and connections had the upper hand. Once the word got in the newspapers and spread across the United States and to Europe, prospectors and investors literally flocked to the area. They were then dependent on local interests who knew the real estate and players in the area. Historically, the earliest of these locals in Florida was Dr. C.A. Simmons of Hawthorn, Florida, around 1877-1889. The primitive mines in Levy and Alucia Counties, outside the great deposits of the Bone Valley, were simply bookmarks and have never played an important role in the history of phosphate mining in Florida. The story really begins with John Dunn, a lawyer and banker operating out of the Merchant Bank and Trust in Ocala. Ocala,

6.1 Bank of Ocala, Florida Department of State

once an important fort town during the Indian removal period and the Seminole Wars, grew into a commercial center for the citrus-growing economy. It incorporated in 1849 and became the Marion County seat. Dunn was a part of that history and growth, and was a major player when the railroad came to Ocala in 1881. Dunn had his hand in the coming economic boom and would be one of the first to know about the railroad. With others, he created the John F. Dunn and Company to form the Bank of Ocala (6.1) in the commercial/merchant center.

The name most associated with the start of the phosphate mining boom in Florida is Albertus Vogt (6.2). Vogt, a transplant to Ocala in 1880, was an employee of Dunn when phosphate was found in neighboring Renfro Springs in 1889. Vogt's history, rarely told, best characterizes the quick buck mentality of Florida in the 1880's. Vogt was born in South Carolina in 1850. His mother and youngest brother died when he was quite young. His father died from injuries sustained in battle. After his father's death, when the Confederate infantry passed by his home in Georgia, Vogt enlisted as an infantryman. He was fourteen years of age, when he suffered serious life-threatening injuries, twice in that year. Upon discharge, he was assigned to the worse prisoner-of-war camp at Andersonville.[2]

6.2 Portrait of Albertus Vogt,
Florida Department of State

I write about Albertus Vogt's early experiences to explain his behaviors in Florida, where he lived in the epicenter of the phosphate rush. Vogt's early years taught him that life was impermanent. What he had as a young man had been taken from him, leaving him to live in the present and spend money as if there were no tomorrow. Vogt went to live with his paternal uncle in Ocala. At thirty-years old he bought a stagecoach company. Four years later, he earned enough to buy property and build a modest home in Renfro Springs. He married a Renfro woman and did what everyone there did, raise crops and grow orange trees. Vogt was no farmer. He had never tended fields or cared for groves. His talents and mindset were best displayed after the war when he joined a guerilla force. Lee may have surrendered at Appomattox, but Vogt and many his age continued to fight to avenge the South.

Vogt found selling real estate more to his skills and more to his desire to make big money, and make it fast. He also had the gift of tongue. Soon he was not only selling properties, but writing articles for major newspapers. Historian, J. Lester Dinkins, based on primary sources, characterized Vogt as unscrupulous in his business transactions. A passionate Confederate, Vogt delighted at cheating Yankees looking for land in Marion County.[3] A photo of Vogt with handle-bar moustache at age 35, reveals in his glance both confidence and sadness. But more than any other character of the mining boom, Vogt was in the right place at the right time. The purest grade of phosphate found to date, was discovered on his ten acres at Renfro Springs. That was April 1889. Vogt took his samples to Ocala and eventually called John Dunn. Dunn took no time hiring a local chemist and making trips to Renfro Springs. In July, Dunn became half-owner of Vogt's ten acres for which he paid Vogt $10,000. More than likely Vogt had purchased the land for no more than $5.00 an acre; the boom was on, Vogt's measly ten acres was worth $20,000. In just five years. Vogt joined forces with Dunn, who had the capital and the connections. Together they worked to purchase all properties in Marion County with phosphate, before the word got out, competitors arrived and land prices skyrocketed. Vogt was to find the properties and negotiate with the property owner. Dunn would supply the capital. Their arrangement was 50/50. Vogt however brought his brother in, John Walker Vogt was promised one half of Vogt's interest.[4] Further southeast along the Peace River in DeSoto County, Florida, phosphate fever was already heating up.

It was a surveyor and cartographer by the name of Francis J. LeBaron who discovered fossil beds and eventually phosphate in the Peace River in 1881.[5] A government surveyor, he was the polar opposite of Albertus Vogt. LeBaron realized the commercial significance to his finds and unsuccessfully attempted to find northern investors to mine the area. The first two, a northern investor, T.S. Moorehead of Pennsylvania who more than likely heard of LeBaron's finds and attempts to recruit capital, joined in business with Confederate Colonel George Washington Scott (6.3). After the slaves were freed, affecting his established cotton plantation near Tallahassee, Florida, Scott was engaged in fertilizers before creating the Arcadia Phosphate Company with Moorehead in 1887. Typical of the post-Civil Wars days, Yankee money worked behind a prominent and respected Confederate partner. Though Scott was born in rural Pennsylvania in 1829, he was now a Southerner. Scott went south after his father's death, in search of

6.3 Portrait of G.W. Scott,
Florida Department of State

health and making his fortune. By all accounts, Scott was not old money. He made his money by working hard, being industrious and saving. This soon to be wealthy businessman built his wealth from scratch over time. Initially he purchased and peddled jewelry and traveled from town-to-town, making friends and staying at great plantations. He finally settled, somewhat, in Tallahassee, Florida, but continued to travel to Georgia. Putting money aside, in 10 years he was able to purchase over 1,408 acres, making him a Southern plantation owner. It was at his Tallahassee plantation where he started experimenting with fertilizers, including phosphate.[6]

When the Civil War broke out, though born in the north, Scott sided and fought with the Confederacy. Records show that he purchased slaves during the war to care for his plantation during his absence. When the war ended Scott was so well-liked that he was voted in as governor, but was soon replaced by the carpetbaggers. Some accounts have Scott purchasing land on the Peace River, way in advance of the fever. This is quite possible, due to the fact that the basis for his success upon moving south was in real estate investment. His Florida phosphate mining revenues were part of a very large portfolio, which included his holding in Georgia: a fertilizer company, a successful mill and a large modern office building. Scott was a rare figure in that he was primarily a fertilizer importer and manufacturer. He brought guano into the United States market and was one of only a few of the pioneers in the phosphate mining boom as a mine owner. Scott was 58 when the money from his phosphate mines started pouring in. He was conservative in his business dealings and definitely not a gambler. Sources reveal, that there was no excitement when Moorehead and Scott began mining in the Peace River. Generally, most could not see a future for phosphate mining there, primarily due to its remote location and the lack of railroads, infrastructure and services. History shows that Moorehead and Scott's investment may have been one of the wisest and most astute in the history of mining phosphate in the United States. The area still has 25% of the world's highest-grade phosphate and is the largest supplier in the world. Scott must have believed in or gotten early information about railroads coming into the area in short order. Then again, with land along the Peace River for as little as $1.50 an acre in 1887, it was not that great of a gamble.

Typical of histories from the 1800's, stories with no basis in fact arise and are retold for generations. One such tall tale appears on the Florida Industrial and Phosphate Research Institute's webpage: *History of Phosphate in Florida.* On the page under the history, it retells a story of two men from Orlando, who while on a hunting trip from Ft. Meade (in Polk County) to Charlotte Harbor, discovered phosphate in 1886.[7] This would have been the same year that Francis LeBaron returned to the same area and three years before Vogt's discovery. The story goes that John C. Jones and Captain W.R. McKee, upon discovering phosphate, orchestrated a scam. They contacted property owners up and down the Peace River, telling them that they found tannic acid in the roots of palmettos, then buying up large tracks for very small amounts. The website credits them with scamming a total of 43 miles of Peace River acreage. I could find no records of these men in Orlando. Their names do appear in Polk County records in an 1880 government census. All accounts of the time show virtually no interest in phosphate in the region or that the area was worth speculating in. Also, a casual hunting trip in the area departing from Orlando seems a bit over the top for 1886. For almost 15 years the prime deposits of high-grade phosphate took a back seat to Marion County and the boom around Dunnellon. It would be years later with the start of the phosphate pebble mining that the second phase of the Florida phosphate mining boom was created.

Back north, Albertus Vogt and his partners were learning the magic of phosphate. At a time when the average wage was 50 cents a day, Vogt and his partners were making $500 a day. In short, even Dunn's purchase of one-half share of Vogt's property for $10,000 was paid for by a month's phosphate shipments. According to historian, David Cook, there were rumors all over the county about Dunn and Vogt keeping their speculations secret. This comment by Dunn leads me to believe that he was a carpetbagger who sought the Vogt's more upstanding investors to front their quick bucks' pursuits. They were successful; with Inglis's investment they brought in E.E.

6.4 Portrait of Captain John L. Inglis 1867,   6.5 Portrait of John L. Inglis,
Florida Department of State   Florida Department of State

Dutton, Philip Lawrey and a Scottish investor, Alexander Wylie. Dunn boasted later that their Dunnellon Phosphate Company had attracted interest from Baltimore and Charleston investors. Initially, with Inglis, capital stock was $1,2000,000. Later they brought in Baldwin Fertilizer of Savannah.

John Livingston Inglis (6.4), not unlike George Washington Scott, was one of those young men of simple means, who moved to Florida in the 1850's to make their fortunes. After all, land was plentiful and cheap as was labor. Inglis arrived in Florida from Scotland in 1857. He had his hand in many industries. Madison County was an agricultural hub. Records show the rice was the leading crop. Inglis soon invested in many ventures as the Florida Manufacturing Company. Inglis was living in Newport, Florida in Wakulla County when the war broke out. Newport was a brand-new town that was built when Port Leon was totally destroyed by a massive hurricane. The region was settled by strong secessionists and Inglis joined their cause. Inglis soon was a sergeant and not long after made captain. His name appears in many war records.

6.6 Portrait of Inglis family, Florida Department of State

We know that Captain Inglis was captured at Nashville, Tennessee on December 19, 1864. Eventually transferred to the Union Prison at Johnson Island, Ohio, when the war ended, he took the oath of allegiance and was released on June 15,1865.

Ocala and Dunn's bank were some distance from Inglis' home and base of Operations. How they met, and just how Dunn was able to involve Inglis in the phosphate mining company is unknown. But in Dunn's own words, he admitted to involving John Inglis in the phosphate mining company, which was critical for optics and his eventual success, "When we had increased our holdings to about 13,000 acres, I invited Capt. John L. Inglis a staunch old Floridian to examine the property, which he did and consented to take an interest in the enterprise."[8]

Dunn later wrote that other prominent people were also invited, but declined. The Dunellon Phosphate Company was finally organized with investments from three more men: E.E. Hutton, Philip Lawtey and Alexander Wylie.[9] In the 1880's Dunn's land investments resulting in the town of Dunnellon bearing his name. The local port town of Inglis, named for his new partner, would imply that mining was not their only mutual concern. Inglis was very active in the Democrat Party and in Florida politics (6.5). Inglis died at the age of 79 in Jacksonville, Florida and was buried by his home in Madison, having lived a full and productive life in his adopted home.

By 1890, Albertus Vogt was living the life. He built his mansion, named Rosebank, with gardens and the finest of furnishings. He traveled extensively, including abroad. His amassed wealth, lived a lavish lifestyle. His fame as the discoverer of phosphate earned him the title, "The Duke of Dunnellon." His articles in the major papers of the time, added to his fame and persona. Vogt was new money and he had all his eggs in one basket. The same year, they had a walk out. A serious labor dispute, probably the only miner's strike of the boom, seriously threatening their production. In 1893, when the financial panic broke out, there was a run on the banks. Dunn's bank was now the Merchant's National Bank of Ocala, and in 1897, Merchant's National became one of the 500 banks in the United States to go bankrupt. Vogt lost $56,000. Desperate from the loss and the death of his wife, Vogt buried oil drums on his Property. When oil oozed out between the rocks of the springs, newspapers declared that Vogt had discovered oil. When that didn't work, he buried gold on his property. In short, these stunts ruined his reputation. He did find an investor for an attempt to mine phosphate in Pasco County, Florida. Initially it looked very promising, but shortly the deposits failed to yield. At the end of his life, he sold his mansion, bought an old resort in Bartow, Florida, making renovations and turning it into a luxury hotel. As an old man, he moved to Jacksonville where he died alone in 1921. A day later his body was transported to a community cemetery in Ocala and buried in an unmarked grave.

Colonel Scott passed away in 1903 in Atlanta, Georgia after a long illness. Scott left behind a legacy of industry and achievement. Later he remarked that he has "been blessed," and soon after he

6.7 French Phosphate Company, Marion County, FL 1890s, Florida Department of State

took his hard-earned money and built a college. At his funeral he was remembered by a loving family and grateful and admiring friends.

The Panic of 1893, ruined Dunn and Vogt's efforts to control phosphate mining in Marion County. British and French companies had always played a significant role in the phosphate boom in the late 1800's. Records show, for instance, a British concern, Wyllie & Gordon had considerable investments in Beaufort County, South Carolina. Charleston had always had strong ties with England, and many Englishmen lent their support to the South during the war.

In 1883, a French mining company bought tracts of land in Citra, just forty miles northeast of Dunnellon (6.7). To guarantee their success, they had built two locomotives. Ciedes Phosphate de France was running by 1894, and phosphate ore was being rapidly mined and taken by rail to Jacksonville. The French company then started mining in Luraville in Suwannee County. No different from the mining operations in South Carolina, phosphate mining was depression proof. Mining operations moved to Live Oak, when the Live Oak and Gulf Railway was completed. Unlike the rail systems elsewhere, the Live Oak and Gulf line was specifically built to haul phosphate. According to historian, Donald Hensley, Jr., the mining company began hauling 20 tons per car and over 450 carloads. By 1896 the railroad hauled out 10,800 tons in 540 cars.[10] (6.8) Mining abruptly stopped when it was determined the phosphate at Live Oak contained too much iron. I stated previously the chemistry could make or break you. Eventually, the Live Oak and Gulf had rail connections with the Plant System and the Florida & Peninsular R.R., and the "New South" was taking hold in Florida.

6.8 Live Oak phosphate rail cars and river barge.
Florida Department of State

ENDNOTES

[1] T.D. Allman, *Finding Florida*, 2013

[2] www.fipr.state.fl.us/about-us/phosphate-primer/discovery-of-phosphate-in-florid

[3] Lester Dinkins, 1969

[4] *Ibid.*

[5] *Ibid.*

[6] https://en.wikipedia.org/wiki/George_Washington_Scott

[7] www.fipr.state.fl.us/about-us/phosphate-primer/discovery-of-phosphate-in-florida/

[8] David Cook, 2011

[9] *Ibid.*

[10] www.taplines.net/feb/loandg2.htm

VII.

LESS FOR MORE

Ultimately, the history of phosphate mining is a study of a failure to set limits; limits as to the scale. This was the heartfelt lesson learned from my work in bioregionalism[1] in the 1990s, and like most important lessons, it is most often realized only in hindsight. Phosphate mining before the middle of the twentieth century was so small in scale, that "intimacy of human and nature"[2] was not threatened. In most cases, the damage was at a scale that the ecology of the mining areas was restorable. Exploring the entire boom epoch in Bone Valley, I was reminded of the lessons learned thirty years prior in the bioregional movement. Prior to his important book on this movement, author Kirkpatrick Sale made life-saving conclusions in an earlier history, *Human Scale.*[3] The following quote from decades ago is, remarkably, very applicable of the phosphate mining in Florida since the 1920s:

So, the technology that does the least alteration of nature, the least harm to other species and systems, and provides the greatest intimacy of human with nature is the best. We could make a scale with that in mind, and judge any technology by its place on that scale.[4]

The phosphate boom changed dramatically going into the twentieth century and then again in present times. The dragline became the symbol of exploitation in the Bone Valley. The explosion of chemical fertilizers used in industrialized counties came about after World War II. As I pointed out in chapter I, phosphate fertilizers mirrored the dramatic changes in agriculture. Those changes could be characterized as less producers on increased acres, in agribusiness as well as mining, more from less.

7.1 Miners with wheel barrows, Florida Department of State

7.2 Power Plant at Hull plant north of Punta Gorda,
Florida Department of State

During the 1920's, phosphate mining in Florida's Bone Valley was transformed by the invention of the dragline. Mining companies that were far fewer in number than the proceeding years were able to mine more acres; more for less. The dragline was invented by John W. Page in 1904 for use in digging the Chicago canal. By 1912, Page realized that building draglines was more lucrative than contracting, so he created the Page Engineering Company in order to build draglines. Page built its first crude walking dragline in 1923 and developed the first diesel engines exclusively for dragline application in 1924. It also invented the arched dragline bucket, a design still used today by modern mining companies. Page's largest dragline was the Model 757 Hinton, Alberta in 1983. It featured a record 75-yard bucket on a 298-foot boom and an operating weight of 4,500 tons.[5]

The development of diesel fueled centrifugal pumps streamlined the mining and processing of phosphate and phosphoric acid. Each critical and essential step in the process was mechanized, resulting in the loss of more jobs. In Bone Valley and other areas, laborers sought jobs in the growing turpentine industry, as jobs related to phosphate processing became fewer and more specialized. Initially, phosphate mining companies shipped crushed phosphate to be sold to companies who would process and market the finished fertilizers. By the 1920's most Florida companies did all the phosphate fertilizer processes and marketing as well.

The history of phosphate mining in the Bone Valley before the 1920's relied heavily on laborers to remove the deep layers of overburden and cart it off. Laborers were paid by the wheelbarrow (7.1). The draglines with their large buckets, soon replaced hundreds of workers. The dragline bucket became the symbol of modern phosphate strip mining in Florida (7.2). Diesel-driven lines proved to be too costly to operate and were soon replaced by electrically driven equipment. Still, in the wilderness areas with no infrastructure, mining companies had to build their own power plants (7.3). The cost of purchasing the new draglines soon eliminated many mining companies who could not afford to modernize their operations, thus mining innovations in the twentieth century led to less but larger phosphate mining companies operating in Florida's Bone Valley. A large dragline system used

7.3 Dragline in operation, Florida Department of State

7.4 Peace River phosphate loading platform, Arcadia. Florida Department of State

in open pit mining costs approximately 50–100 million dollars. A typical bucket has a volume ranging from 40 to 80 cubic yards, though extremely large buckets have ranged up to 5,900 cu feet; the length of the boom ranges from 148 to 328 feet. In a single cycle, it can move up to 450 tons of material.[6] (7.4)

The diesel tractor, equally replaced workers for the removal of the coverings of the soil and the tilling to prepare for seeding the plants. The increase in agricultural production fueled the advancements in the mining of phosphates for fertilizers.

Florida led the world in the mining processes and innovations of the twentieth- century. The wet process was developed for the production of phosphate acid. It required a large quantity of water, referred to as process water, used to make the slurry. The large amounts of process water that holds the heat produced in the processing is eventually released into the atmosphere through evaporation while cooling in storage ponds at the site. In the early twenty-first century, it was reported that phosphate giant Mosaic was using 17.7 billion gallons of Florida groundwater, 2.2 billion gallons more than the entire volume of the regional reservoir.[7] The first decades of phosphate mining in the south employed great numbers of laborers to process the phosphate. More water replaced the workers and increased the demands on the environment.

By the 1920's, Florida's Bone Valley had experienced dramatic changes, first in the number of mining companies. There were fewer companies but more acres being mined. This mirrored farming, fewer farmers were farming larger tracks of land. Even before 1920, improvements in mining had resulted in consolidation. At the height of the mining boom in the Peace River Valley, there were over 215 separate mining companies. By 1905, there were only 50. In 1900, it took a year to mine a 15-acre mine site with hundreds of miners using picks, shovels and wheelbarrows. In the river, steam dredges could extract phosphate pebbles that could not be exploited by laborers. Mining companies employed labor-saving centrifugal pumps, mounted to the barges. On land, phosphate pebbles and hard rock at depths of 15 to 20 feet could be mined with the invention of the steam shovel. To show the radical change in

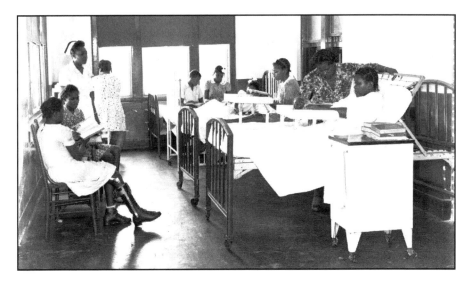

*7.5 African-American children's ward of Brewster mining town,
Florida Department of State*

productivity, one steam shovel operated by three men replaced 80 men with picks and shovels. Correspondingly, in order to compete, mining companies sought out more and more acres.

Even into the twentieth-century, many of the phosphate producing mines in Bone Valley were far from the nearest town or commercial center. The building of miner quarters and housing that dated back to the plantation owners gone mining in Beaufort County, S.C., evolved into the building of modern mining towns along the Peace River in central Florida. One such town, the town of Brewster, was built for the workers by the American Cyanamid Corporation in 1910 (7.5). The company built homes, schools, a movie theater, medical clinic, post office, and swimming pool. Due to the Jim Crow laws, that remained in Florida till the 1960's, the company actually built two towns, one for whites south of the mine and one for blacks on the eastside of the mine. When the company closed their operations in 1960, workers could buy their homes from the company or it would be torn down. After 1976, American Cyanamid deeded the property to the state in partial payment of a long-standing judgement against the company for environmental damage. Brewster was one of dozens of mining towns built and then abandoned by the 1960's (7.6).

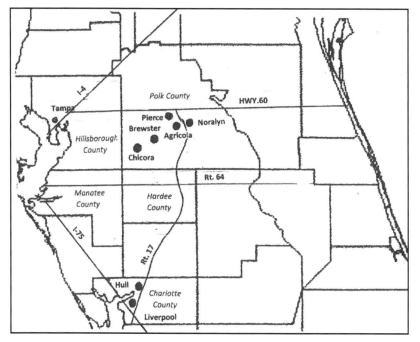

7.6 *Map of mining ghost towns in the Bone Valley, Ted Ehmann*

The only reason we know about the history of phosphate mining in Florida in the first half of the twentieth century is because of the testimony and report of a phosphate prospector, Wayne Thomas, at a special Congressional hearing in Lakeland, Florida on November 28, 1937.[8] You might wonder why Congress was having a hearing about phosphates in Florida? It was to address soil fertility concerns of President Franklin D. Roosevelt(7.7). Those concerns came after the devasting Dust Bowl, caused largely by the federal government, which tried to correct the situation beginning with the Soil Conservation and Domestic Allotment Act of 1936: P.L. 74-46 (February 26, 1936).[9] It was designed to support farm income by making soil-conservation and soil-building payments to participating farmers. It reduced surpluses by paying farmers for shifting from crops in excess supply (soil depleting crops) to soil building crops like legumes and grasses. This law, as amended, continues to serve as the enabling authority for a number of activities and programs carried out by the Natural Resources Conservation Service.

7.7 F.D.R. in 1937, Wikimedia

Another New Deal program during the Great Depression was the Tennessee Valley Authority. The authority had for a brief period been involved in the very lucrative phosphate mining which began in Tennessee the same time as in Florida. Few people outside of Tennessee knew that in the middle counties, there were forty phosphate mining companies in 1900. When Roosevelt studied phosphates used for fertilizers in the United States, of course, Florida's industry and reserves came up. So did the fact that historically the U.S. was exporting those reserves to foreign nations. On May 20, 1938, Roosevelt delivered a special message to Congress on soil fertility.[10] He stated that the nation should adopt a national policy for the production and conservation of phosphates. (7.8) It was the first-time phosphates had been politicized. Congress followed suite and passed Public Resolution 112 which called for an investigation into the adequacy and uses of U.S. phosphate reserves, the largest being by far in Florida. At one point some people actually proposed making it unlawful to export Florida's phosphates. Knowing today that Florida's reserves are very limited, it is not inconceivable to see our government attempt to limit export at some future time.

The key witness before the Congressional Hearing on "phosphate adequacy and reserves" in phosphate rich Florida was a Mr. Wayne Thomas, a resident of Hillsborough County. From his resumé at the time, it was clear why he was the most qualified to speak on the subject. A resident of Florida since 1904, Thomas's business was the discovery, development and even sale of phosphate properties. Since his boyhood in Bartow, he had studied seven large phosphate mines of his time there in Polk County. The twelve years before testifying that day to Congress, he prospected phosphate lands extensively in Polk, Hillsborough, Manatee, Hardee, Lake, Pasco,

Hernando, and other counties. Also important, he knew all the people in the field, From foremen and field crews, sharing maps and notes. With such an incredible resumé, it would be difficult to question his authority, as well as refute his figures. Here is his assessment of the acres being mined in Florida in 1938:

AMERICAN AGRICULTURAL CHEMICAL CO	52,085
INTERNATIONAL AGRICULTURAL CORPORATION	44,070
AMERICAN CYANAMID CO	20,140
PHOSPHATE MINING CO	16,480
CORONET PHOSPHATE CO	13,116
SOUTHERN PHOSPHATE CORPORATION	11,360
SWIFT & CO.	6,630
TOTAL	**163,881**[11]

The total acreage owned by those companies was 163,881. The reserves they have prospected and included in the above estimates cover less than 80,000 acres. In addition to the reporting companies, there are these inactive companies which by the same standards have a total of 250,000,000 tons of pebble rock:

ACREAGE OWNED ARMOR FERTILIZER WORKS.	2,560
BAUGH CHEMICAL	2,760
BRADLEY ESTATES, INC	10,190
DAVISON CHEMICAL CO.	2,125
DOMINION PHOSPHATE CO	653
FLORIDA PHOSPHATE MINING CO. (ROYSTER)	1,670
PEMBROKE CHEMICAL CO	1,230
POLK PHOSPHATE CO	5,315
TENNESSEE CORPORATION	2,760

TILGHMAN (INDEPENDENT CHEMICAL CO. _____	4,820
VIRGINIA-CAROLINA CHEMICAL CO _____	18,545
TOTAL _____	**52,628** [12]

Since the 1950s, these mines have been for the most part abandoned. Large mining companies like Swift & Company have picked up and left. As was the need in the twentieth century, companies like American Cyanamid built entire towns for their employees next to the mines and processing plants. Just ten miles south of Mulberry, Florida is what remains of a large town built by American Cyanamid in 1910 for their phosphate workers and their families. It is one of dozens of ghost towns in the Bone Valley. Today, rather than preserving the past, property owner Mosaic Company is using barbed wire to fence off what remains from trespassers. For many years this large ghost town has attracted many visitors and curiosity seekers.

7.8 Mining town of Brewster, Florida Department of State

7.9 Employees honored for years of service, Florida Department of State

Uninhabited since 1960, the town of Brewster (7.9) was founded in 1910 and for decades flourished from phosphate mining. It was largely a typical southern, segregated mining town. The town had its own schools, movie theater, medical clinic and post office, which was established in 1913 and discontinued in 1961. Brewster even had its own community swimming pool. Some accounts state that it had approximately 163 houses and at one time a population of 2,500. The town's most famous hometown boy was John V. Atanasoff, the inventor of the digital computer, who grew up there. The village was officially closed down by the company in 1962. Much of Brewster was demolished at the time, but some abandoned buildings remain, including a smokestack which rises prominently in the area as a landmark. A sign of things to come, the deed to Brewster was turned over to the state of Florida in partial payment of a judgment against American Cyanamid for environmental damages.

7.10 Mining town of Nichols, Florida Department of State

Then again, what reparations were made to the hundreds of workers and their families who were jobless when American Cyanamid and the dozens of other companies pulled out of Bone Valley by the end of the twentieth-century?

Village life characterized the miner's life from its earliest days in Bone Valley. The earliest of these villages was at Tiger Bay near Fort Meade, which was built by the Palmetto Phosphate Company. The town of Nichols (7.9), built by the Virginia-Carolina Chemical Company, consisted of about 120 houses and dates to the 1920s. Other company installations included Pierce, built in 1906 by the American Agricultural Chemical Company; Ridgewood, built by Davison Chemical Company; a group of houses near Bartow built by Armour Fertilizer Company; and a large number of homes near Mulberry, built by International Minerals and Chemicals Company.

Rents were very reasonable. The company also provided all the basic utilities and services. It was a big difference from the late nineteenth century, when you could 'owe your soul to the company store.' Safety was also a major benefit. Even into the twentieth century violence and lawlessness persisted in the remote areas of central Florida. There was no safety net when you were too old or sick to work. Only employees could rent in the village. Upon retirement, no matter how long you worked for the company, you were forced to move. Needless to say, company houses were in demand, and there was always a waiting list.

When the unions in the 1930's negotiated their early contracts, it led to the elimination of company commissaries and villages. The villages did not completely phase out. However, when the phosphate mines expanded their operations rapidly in the 1950's, men no longer worked next to the mines. Families began to move to nearby cities where there were more opportunities. As the need for company towns waned, the companies sold the houses to workers at reasonable rates and moved the homes to nearby communities.

By the end of the twentieth century, the few large mining companies in the highly competitive but lucrative Florida phosphate industry sought more with less, and were using contract laborers. Gone were the days of being a company man and being rewarded for your years of service (7.10) 1n 2019, half of Mosaic's 7,000 jobs were performed by contract labor.

By 1960, Floridians were learning the hard lessons of less being more. More advances in mining technology meant fewer workers. More advances meant more mining by fewer companies. During the Reagan years, the decade experienced a great deal of affluence, corporate wealth and a propensity for deregulation. The decade prior brought into being an age of environmental protection. The decade between 1970 and 1980 is now known as the "Environmental Decade." If your business was at cause for pollution of our air and water, regulations were put in place and a whole new government agency was created to

7.11 President Nixon signing the new environmental laws, Library of Congress

enforce the new environmental laws and regulations. The 1970's and 80's saw larger mining companies and expanded mining lands using massive amounts of water. Phosphate mining processes, being water dependent, meant being near creeks, springs, rivers and wetlands in Florida; thus miners were potentially major polluters.

On January 1,1970, President Nixon signed the National Environmental Policy Act. (7.11) Later that year, Nixon created the E.P.A., the department that would enforce his new environmental agenda. The primary focus of the new legislation and agency was pollutants. Clean air, surface water, ground water and the disposal of solid wastes were prioritized. Included early on was the pollution of ground water from chemicals used in agriculture. It was the first time in American history that agricultural chemicals, as well as pollution and contamination from mining, were monitored and regulated. Industries were forced to invest in technology and processes in order to operate and meet the government-imposed standards.[13]

A year later, the first phosphate mining accident occurred in Bone Valley. I know because I live in Charlotte County at the mouth of the Peace River, where the toxins killed shell fish and the ecology still suffers 47 years later. A very large pond containing the process water and toxic clay and minerals was released during a bad storm, when the water increased and the dike burst. There was no appropriate riparian buffer and the ponds contents were released up river at the IMC Fort Meade, then carried by the flood-swollen Peace River down to the Gulf.

Advances like the drag line left the landscape looking like a weird moonscape of stripped barren acres with rising gypsum stacks. Florida made no attempts to force the mining companies to pay to have the landscape in Bone Valley reclaimed. The new E.P.A., which protected wetlands like those that comprise the Peace River region, were forced by federal law in 1975 to reclaim, on an acre for acre and environment type for type. Here is where Mr.Wayne Thomas's testimony in 1938 helps.

The majority of corporations who mined during the twentieth century simply closed down their mines, leaving the reclamation to the state with funds from the sale of the acreage.

In 1974, the Florida Legislature finally dealt with the issue of reclamation. They passed a law requiring all phosphate mining companies, after July of 1975, to properly restore the acres mined. Known as Chapter 378, Florida's exacting reclamation standards and timelines 62C-36.008, mirrored laws proposed in other states.[14] These long-needed laws were passed in the spirit of the environmental times, and in response to the new priorities put forth by Congress and the Nixon administration. Florida imposed a tax on phosphate in order to pay for the reclamation.

However, the law involved only mining after July of 1975 and not the over 250,000 acres strip mined during the previous 75 years. The intent of the new law was to make mining companies responsible for literally restoring the once strip-mined lands to their original state, thereby they would serve as they had for generations as productive lands for multiple uses, and not abandoned wastelands. For instance websites of both the FIPR Institute and Mosaic Company show photos of reclaimed lands returning to orchards. As time passed the lands in the Bone Valley were not in demand, but as the demand for developable land in Florida increased, that would soon change.

The New York Times holds the record on negative stories about the environmental and health hazards apparent with Florida's phosphate mining. An example was an article written by Wayne King that appeared July 24, 1976. The headline read, "Florida Phosphate Pollution Stirs Alarm."[15] The article exposes air pollution, but takes the opportunity to paint the mining industry in Florida with a broad brush; radiation was now a new health risk from the phosphate mining:

> The radiation hazard is the latest and most dramatic of the environmental concerns that have caused alarm in Florida about the strip mining and processing of phosphate. The industry is also the target of vocal criticism on other issues that touch virtually every facet of life in Florida: air pollution, water pollution and depletion and destruction of land. [16]

Three years later, in 1978, the state of Florida took on the large mining companies, not for environmental claims, but the issue of mining rights to Florida's national forests. It was the first time since the boom in the late 1880's that the state expressed displeasure and took the companies to court. As reported in the March 11, 1978 *New York Times*:

> The State of Florida, disturbed by phosphate mining on disputed land and the prospect of strip mines in a national forest, is fighting with the industry over the use of thousands of acres in the world's richest phosphate reserves. For nearly a century, the industry mined phosphate rock from central Florida with little Government interference. Recently, however, the state has doubled the mineral severance tax, restricted claims to sovereign land and entered a complex lawsuit contending that seven concerns have been removing phosphate and uranium ore from state-owned river-beds without state approval and without paying royalties.[17]

Historically, the issue of strip-mining phosphate in the national forests got the attention of the first environmental group. The Audubon Society had a hearing with the U.S. Department of the Interior. Audubon's organized protest foreshadowed those of the Sierra Club and others twenty-five years later. The legal battle went unnoticed by the people of Florida, who were dealing with the gas lines and other problems related to the Carter years.

As if by some strange coincidence, the same year that the State of Florida went to court with the phosphate mining companies over land rights, the state created the Florida Industrial Phosphate Research Institute. Billed and funded as an independent state agency, the non-profit institute was charged with conducting research in the following areas: mining and beneficiation; their website states that: The FIPR Institute's research in the areas of mining and beneficiation (mineral processing) concentrates on issues pertaining to the mining of phosphate rock and beneficiation of phosphate ore (matrix), which separates the valuable phosphate rock from waste clay and sand. According to the FIPR Institute's legislative mandate, the Institute's research should develop technology to help Florida's phosphate industry become more efficient and environmentally sound.

In hindsight, three important realities are strikingly absent in the founding documents and the stated mission of the new agency. Seven years prior, the Florida phosphate mining industry, specifically IMC, was responsible for the Peace River accident. To not mandate FIPRI with the research and development of environmental safeguards and good practices was a huge oversight. Second, the reference to the "industry" implied that there would always be many companies mining phosphates in Florida. This faulty assumption lacked an understanding of the trend in the industry since the nineteenth century. Namely that there had been repeated consolidation, that significantly and predictably resulted in fewer and fewer companies over time. By the twenty-first century, over 85% of all phosphate mining was by a single company, Mosaic. Therefore, today FIPRI is a government agency conducting research and improving processes for a single company. Objectivity and independent research no longer exist. In researching for this book, for instance, all major facts and statistics supplied by the agency per my requests, were produced by Mosaic's public relations department. The third important reality missing in the charter for the agency is the depletion of Florida's phosphate reserves. Phosphate reserves are not renewable. The fixed amounts suitable for mining have an end date. Common sense would dictate that the single agency involved with the phosphate industry would be concerned (research) with the amount of phosphate still available, and in their best estimate, when those remaining deposits will be depleted. They were not.

Before any in the public were made aware in the late 1970's of the FIPRI, the new agency, their current websites states further that:

> As phosphate mining moves south from the Bone Valley mining core in Polk County, the land has much more dolomite (calcium magnesium carbonate), which causes problems when the phosphate is processed

into the phosphoric acid used in fertilizers. This has made finding ways to separate the dolomite from the phosphate a research priority for the FIPR Institute.[18]

One would think that as in the past, going back to the South Carolina lowlands, the research and development would be the responsibility of the mining companies. Florida has its own way of doing business. The following from the FIPRI website proves that the institute is merely a puppet for the industry players.

It is important to note that the institute's research was and remains, information only, and does not result in policy regulations and enforcement. Phosphogypsum, a significantly environmentally harmful by-product of processing phosphates for use as fertilizers, was one of the institute's primary areas of focus. Finding commercial uses for the stacks, while a noble pursuit, has proven to be fruitless. Likewise, minimizing the environmental harm caused by the large quantities of acidic process water circulated around the gypsum stacks, remains unsolved.

Another noble pursuit, once the responsibility by law of a dozen or more companies, reclamation, now remains the responsibility of the one remaining player, Mosaic. The institute states the following about their research and success with reclamation of mined land in Florida:

> Since opening, the Institute has funded research to find out what it takes to reclaim lakes, streams, wetlands, dry uplands, scrub habitat, forested areas, and phosphatic clay settling areas. This includes studying wildlife, vegetation, hydrology, and soils. The FIPR Institute's reclamation research also addresses phosphogypsum stack closure issues such as economical and effective ways to establish vegetation on the stacks. The FIPR Institute has also studied ways to use reclaimed lands for agricultural purposes and has put on a number of symposiums and conferences related to all reclamation issues.[19]

7.12 Kevin Erwin, Senior Ecologist, Florida, Courtesy of Kevin Erwin

Reclamation has been an area where the law of diminishing returns is ever-apparent. Before the removal of the overburden, the marsh grasses, trees, shrubs and wildlife, the acreage was pristine wetlands that were a part of the larger ecosystem. So, imagine the cost to restore in kind and type all of what was originally there in the manner that the area worked within the larger ecological system prior to strip mining. Kevin Erwin, (7.12) a Certified Senior Ecologist, wrote about the cost of reclamation in 2003. In 2003 the estimated amount per acre was $25,000.[20] With inflation that means that the cost to reclaim in 2018 was $34,719.87 an acre. He has testified FIPRI's guidelines and estimates have proven to be inaccurate and inappropriate. IMC's history thus far in Bone Valley has been poor at best.

Reclamation is the most important issue for Florida in the twenty-first century. Erwin's testimony can be read by accessing *An Analysis if IMC Reclamation Costs for the Proposed Ona Mine*, FIPRI, 2004, and his findings are applicable to all current and future mining by Mosaic in Florida. Erwin stated:

> In my evaluation of approximately fifty IMC reclamation projects in 2003, I have observed no improvement in conditions since the completion of our study for Florida Institute of Phosphate Research

(FIPR) in 1997 entitled Evaluation of Constructed Wetlands on Phosphate Mined Lands in Florida. This presents a risk that I believe is now associated with the goal of successful reclamation by IMC. Success cannot be assured and substantially effects the costs of reclamation. Furthermore, the very poor conditions I observed on most of IMC's reclamation projects mean that their methods and budgets for management and monitoring is suspect and require significant review and modification.[21]

Here, the state of Florida, our elected officials and appointed bureaucrats must face the facts. The deposits of phosphate commercially viable in central Florida peaked in the first decade of the twenty-first century. To continue to fund research in processes, when there is no future, makes no sense. All funds must be directed to cleaning up and reclaiming after the 120 years of strip mining. None of these officials have been truthful to Florida's residents. In 2001 the legislature created a huge fund under the Forever Florida Act 259.105,[22] in order to buy precious wilderness and wetlands for preservation. Every year since, they take those funds to undo the dams, dikes and water diversion projects in the northern Everglades, billions of dollars-worth of projects that resulted in the eventual destruction of the Florida Everglades. Where are, or where will be the funds to reclaim over 250,000 acres in need of reclamation from the mining? There no longer exists a pool of a dozen or more large companies now mining phosphate and responsible for reclamation. Mosaic, that last player when the corporation first formed in 2004, immediately took the increased assets to set up operations in Brazil and Saudi Arabia.[23] It is not like they are making a future in Bone Valley; quite the opposite.

FIPRI was created by the state during the twenty years of the phosphate mining speculation and boom that started in the late 1990's. A USGS report produced by geologist Richard Jasinski, stands in stark contrast to the size and scope of the industry today. In terms of the viability of the 1978 created Florida Industrial Phosphate Research Institute, the industry in Florida has made them obsolete. There is no longer a need to research all of those

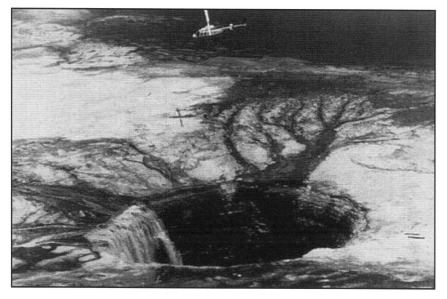

7.13 Mulberry Sink Hole, Florida D.E.P.

areas except for one, reclamation. Reclamation would be best researched and staffed by environmental specialists and trained ecologists like Kevin Erwin. This reality is underscored by their response to my request for present-day statistics being answered by Mosaic and not the Institute.

Until 2000, Florida has been the epicenter of America's phosphate production since the late 1800s, when phosphate rock was discovered along the Peace River. The skeletons and waste products of creatures living in primeval seas were deposited in Central Florida, an area now rich in fossils and phosphate that became known as Bone Valley. One hundred companies once mined the rock around Lakeland, Mulberry, Bartow and Plant City. The number of mining companies slid to about 30 by 1970 and less than a dozen by 2000 as the strong gobbled up the weak, more for less. There was widespread speculation about how much is available in existing reserves. A few years ago, economists, sustainability advocates and mineral-mining experts started crunching numbers. The results were scary. Rather than honesty, Mosaic Company spends millions in public relations to communicate a rosy future and that all is well.

7.14 Noralyn Plant closed, Florida Department of State

In 1994, a 180-foot-deep sinkhole opened in a "gyp stack" near Mulberry, (7.13) draining acidic holding water into the aquifer that supplies drinking water to millions of residents in the Tampa Bay area. The accident caused 50 million gallons of contaminated acidic process water to pour from a retention pond into the Alafia River, killing hundreds of acres of vegetation and millions of fish.[24] In 2004, hurricane-whipped winds churned waves of water over a pile in Riverview, spilling 65 million gallons of acidic wastewater into Tampa Bay and destroying large numbers of crabs, shrimp and fish, 150 acres of mangroves and 22 acres of sea grass. If the residents of Florida needed proof that all that funding for a state institute to research and solve that exact issue was money wasted, they got it!

I have not said much about the economics of the phosphate market, of upturns and downturns in supply and demand. After World War II, similar to other global commodities, phosphate had its good days and bad days. By the very end of the twentieth century, the global phosphate market was facing a down turn. Before American Cyanimide closed its Brewster plant,[25] International Mining Company (IMC) built a large, state-of-the arts modern phosphate processing plant near Bartow in 1950. Citing global supply and demand imbalances, company president Steven Demetrious announced 49 years later that they were reducing the company's output to two-thirds. Hundreds of employees were laid off and eventually lost their jobs when the Noralyn plant closed in 1999.[26] (7.14) Noralyn stated that their mine would be closed for seven months, but looking back, the report by the USGS verified that there was an upturn in the phosphate market at that time. Also, in a report by Richard Jasinski for the USGS, he documented that two years before IMC shut down three plants in Florida's Bone Valley, they applied for permits and rights to operate in two new areas in the south, the Pine Level and Ona mines.[27]

In 1999, *The Chicago Tribune* published an article on the cut backs by IMC in phosphate "That pride is not without justification." The cut backs they stated were due to decreased demand from the agriculture market. In Hillsborough County, the phosphate industry and related shipping concerns pump billions of dollars into the local economy through the trade in ammonium phosphate, by providing American farmers with 75% of their fertilizer needs. The paper reported that "Florida phosphate is a chief reason why food prices in this country remain relatively low."[28] In Chapter I, I reported the finding of historians of American farming. Chemical fertilizers increased farming cost and thereby food costs. They forced farmers to increase acreage, as well as rely on problematic farming practices simply to stay afloat. IMC's assertions then and Mosaic's today, that crop yields made possible by increased chemical fertilizers keep prices low[29] is simply false. They also do not take into account the expensive damage to the environment which, when factored into production, gives you the true cost.

One of the only statements by the Sierra Club that I have agreed with since they have taken on the phosphate mining industry in Florida is the fact that Florida, which has gotten the least benefits from 135 years of mining phosphates, will be forced to pay one hundred percent of the cost for the environmental damage for supplying the world with is phosphate. If you believe Senior Ecologist Kevin Erwin, and I do, that cost to restore, type-by-type, the ecologies in ruin and avoid an ecological crisis, would most-likely bankrupt the state and it's residents.

ENDNOTES

Ibid.

[1] https en.wikipedia.org/wiki/Bioregionalis

[2] Kirkpatrick Sale, *Dwellers in the Land...*, 2000

[3] Kirkpatrick Sale, *Human Scale*, 2019

[4] *Ibid.*

[5] https://en.wikipedia.org/wiki/Dragline_excavator

[6] *Ibid.*

[7] *The Bradenton Times*, Editorial, "The Hidden Tax on Phosphate Mining," Sept. 8, 2011

[8] Bob Hurst, April 19, 2009, shnv.blogspot.com/2009/04/two-giants-of-their-times.html

[9] https://en.wikipedia.org/wiki/Soil_Conservation_and_Domestic_Allotment_Act_of_1936

[10] Special Congressional Hearing, Lakeland, FL Nov. 28, 1937, Report, pubs. usgs.gov/bul/0934/report.pdf

[11] *Ibid.*

[12] *Ibid.*

[13] https://en.wikipedia.org/wiki/United_States_Environmental_Protection_Agency

[14] www.leg.state.fl.us/statutes Chapter 378

[15] Wayne King, *New York Times*, 1976

[16] *Ibid.*

[17] https://www.nytimes.com/1978/06/11/archives/florida-battling-phosphate-industry-over-mining.html

[18] www.fipr.state.fl.us

[19] *Ibid.*

[20] Kevin Erwin, editorial, 2003

[21] Kevin Erwin, 2004

[22] www.leg.state.fl.us/statutes

[23] www.mosaicco.com

[24] Joel Hruskz, Sept. 23, 2016, www.extremetech.com/extreme/236163-how-a-massive-sinkhole-dumped-200-million-gallons-

[25] ghosttowns.com/state/fl/brewster.html

[26] www.abandonedfl.com/noralyn-phosphate-mine/

[27] Richard Jasinski, ww.usgs.gov/centers/nmic/phosphate-rock-statistics-and-information

[28] George Gunset, *Chicago Tribune*, Nov. 12, 1999

[29] www.croplife.com/crop-inputs/fertilizer/

VIII.

TOO MUCH IS TOO MUCH

The fevered pace of strip mining the phosphate rock and pebbles in the Bone Valley for the past 135 years should draw attention to what many would consider to be far more important, that being Florida's natural habitat. It is not just an emotional argument either. Phosphate reserves are limited and not renewable. The history of phosphate mining in Florida is one of a laisse-faire involvement by the state up until the 1970s. Except for the brief scuffle between the state of Florida and the mining companies in 1978 over land rights,[1] phosphate mining in Florida had few opponents and no competing interest for most of those years. Recently I found a research paper by Leah Holst. Holst discovered that at the very time of mechanization in phosphate mining, public outcry and lawsuits over water pollution due to phosphate mining started as early as 1911. Her exhaustive research found a steady stream of legal challenges to phosphate mining operations and mine waste storage issues regarding water from 1911 to 1975, when the first national standards for water and air were introduced. Likewise, air pollution outrage and lawsuits were consistent from 1944 to 1975. To quote Holst:

> Citizen complaints and legal action regarding water pollution from the mines occurred despite the steady flow of mining protests, most legislation aimed to pacify the citizen outrage and allowing mining companies to continue without major limits imposed.[2]

The phosphate mining boom was and remains today a major piece of the history of the Sunshine State. That this book is the very first to capture this history is truly amazing. Brief histories authored by the Mosaic mining company or the state-funded institute that supports them is all that are available to the public; and such brief histories are biased and self-serving narratives. The first historian to include anything about Florida's phosphate mining was T.D. Allman in 2013. In his history, *Finding Florida,* Allman shows its beginnings and brings phosphate mining and environmental issues forward:

> In 1880 Florida produced no phosphate, in 1888 just 3,000 tons. By 1898, thanks to the development of diesel and electric-driven extraction devices, nearly 600,000 ton were extracted. The figure was 860,000 tons in1903, more than a million tons just one year later. Back then it took a year for the phosphate companies to strip fifteen acres. Today it takes a month, and the production figures show it. By 2003, more than 20 million tons of phosphate rock were being ripped out of Florida every year, devastating vast stretches of central Florida.

Allman continues to go right to one very obvious environmental impact of all that mining, a by-product being more than "one billion tons of radioactive phosphor-gypsum littering the state."[3] As historian Kirkpatrick Sale would label, the results of exploitation of the environment without limits.[4]

When I reached out to the historical societies in the Bone Valley mining communities, none had archived or concerned themselves with this history. One historian, even argued against the notion that there ever was a phosphate boom at all. As an author of what I refer to as Florida's forgotten histories, historically Florida's history beginning after the Civil War is one that is invented and created to attract people to a Florida with no basis in fact. As far these local historians go, out of sight is out of mind. They must have grown up and currently live where there are few, if any, reminders of 135 years of strip mining, which is pretty much everyone.[5]

While the 135 years of extracting record tonnage of phosphate from central Florida has resulted in many environmental crises, this book shares the cultural impacts. I am attempting to put a human face on the phosphate mining boom, then and now. For decades, communities have preserved and now display Florida's railroad history. True, it was the railroads that made the many land booms and the resulting populating of "paradise" possible. The story of Florida sacrificing its lands for the world's farming with nothing to show for it, I believe is a much more compelling history, a history not shared with any other state in the nation, nor most areas in the world.

The merger of the two major mining companies to form Mosaic in October, 2004 continues to have a profound effect on the state's fragile mid-section. Even before the ink was dry on the merger agreement, the new global giant bought interest in two other countries. In a response to the government's study of the few remaining economically viable deposits remaining in Florida, I.M.C.'s permit applications for the "southern phosphate districts" in Bone Valley became a priority. Unlike prior phosphate mining extensions, there was immediate opposition by the counties down river, as well as state and national environmental groups. A series of lawsuits were filed and the new battle lines to halt the permits for the southern deposits were drawn. The rivers and aquifer were the rallying points in a new age of environmental pushback. Many believed that it was too much, and were ready to fight back. It has been, all these years now, a full frontal attack on the mining permits. All the time, a series of strict regulations passed by the state, 62C-36.008, Reclamation Standards of October 16,1987 were their best offense.

Since the 1980's ecologist Kevin Erwin has been observing the attempts by Florida's phosphate mining companies to restore completely the areas mined to their original ecologies. His conclusion has been that all attempts have failed (8.1). Erwin wrote an editorial based on his studies in 2004. He concluded, "In 2003, I evaluated 50 IMC reclamation projects. I have observed no improvement in conditions since the completion of our 1997 study for the Florida Institute of Phosphate Research... In short, neither its budgets nor its methods are working-and they haven't for years."[6]

It is not just a case of filling in the mines and planting things. There are intricate relationships between uplands and wetlands. Restoration requires that the exact habitat, water, soil, plant

8.1 Current attempt at reclamation, Florida E.P.A.

and animals are returned. It is not landscaping and requires the kind of local knowledge that left when the Indians were removed. According to Erwin: "The strip- mining process completely alters soils and hydrology. Strip mining's complete disturbance of the land represents a significant challenge to restore the nature system type by type, function by function."[7]

Restoring the functionality of any part of an entire system is an overwhelming process. It is also very expensive, sometimes, according to Kevin Ewin, as much as 11 times more than budgeted by the companies and the E.P.A. Erwin's review of the IMC's estimated cost per acre revealed it was just a fraction of what needed to be paid to restore the connectivity, or repair the un-connectivity, of the mined area. For every reclamation project, IMC paid under half of the approximate amount needed to restore the earth contouring. No money was spent for shaping (8.2). Erwin, an ecologist, estimates that one IMC reclamation of woodland pasture type should have cost $22,000, yet IMC had no monies for the important part of the project. In fact, IMC's cost was only $5,453.00 for a reclamation that in 2003 should have cost $39,118.00.

Therefore, the mining company has not been reclaiming type by type. The specific contours and shaping to reclaim the connectivity of the specific woodland pasture site were not tended to.[8]

All past efforts at reclamation have been failures from the beginning. No one took the time to understand at an ecological system's view, what was there before it was all dug up. How can you put a system back together, above and below ground, if you never recorded the system before you took it apart. Modern phosphate mining digs down 100 to 200 feet, taking out layer upon layer of area specific strata of sand, mineral, clay and rock. Over millions of years, the area functioned specifically. Most important to restoring the land later is permeability. When you dig up entire regions, all the layers, mix them up and throw them back in the hole, they cannot function as they did prior. In fact, Erwin states that they are lost lands and will never function again (8.2). The mined areas should be returned to the condition of the area you see adjoining it.

Erwin told me that after some forty years of reviewing reclaimed lands from phosphate strip mining, he has many important unanswered questions. Critical questions that the state and federal

8.2 Strange landscape unfamiliar to the Florida interior, Florida E.P.A.

agencies should be asking. Now that 30% of the state has been deep mined, a really big question is what happens below the surface, which afterwards had the mix thrown back in the holes? What happens with water retention, permeability and the immense aquifer down below, involving the ecology of 30% of the state's lands?[9] When I left Erwin's office, all I could think was, here was a case for cloning. Kevin is a consulting company of one and to avoid environmental disaster, if that is even realistically possible in Florida, we need dozens of people with his skills, experience and the critical questions.

Environmentalists and worse, well-meaning environmental groups like the Sierra Club, are clueless when it comes to the critical issues surrounding mining land reclamation. They have spent their time, energy and money fighting such things as life-sustaining elements like carbon, creating fear over natural changes in climate, and saving one species temporarily, so much so that they have no concept of the big picture. Their lack of ecological understanding has rendered them useless.[10] True, the Sierra Club is right to call attention to both the effects of the mining over decades and the new mines in the south, related to wetlands, ground water and the Florida aquifer; but if they wish to stop it, they have one chance currently, the pocketbook. If the governments, agencies and people demand they pay the true cost of "type by type" reclamation, Mosaic and others may simply walk away. After all my research, I can totally agree with a post on the Florida Sierra Club webpage of July 30, 2012 asserting that all "recognize that Florida phosphate mining is not necessary for US or world fertilizer production and that Florida mining is being subsidized by Florida taxpayers and the Florida environment."[11]

I believe that with authorities like Kevin Erwin a fairly accurate dollar amount can be calculated for that subsidy. In the critical years when Sierra Club knew that permits were being reviewed for the southern mining extensions into Hardee and DeSoto Counties, they could have stopped the process by showing the commissioners that Mosaic was not offering near enough money for required contouring and shaping in their reclamation cost proposals. That opportunity, at least to stop the Hardee County mining extension was lost in January of 2019,[12] when the county approved the plans.

As of late 2019, there was still an opportunity for DeSoto, but Mosaic is seriously challenging their decision.[13]

Studies performed in the late 1990's highlighted the diminishing reserves of phosphate.[14] IMC, International Mining Corporation, a major fertilizer company, applied for permits to mine over 20,000 acres of wetlands adjoining the Peace River in the southernmost areas of the Bone Valley deposits (8.3). It was business as usual, or so they thought. That same year, immediately after the Department of Environmental Protection issued a notice of intent to issue the permits for the new 20,675 acre mine in Ona and IMC's plan for reclamation when they finish, a court action was filed. Peace River v IMC Phosphates was a joint law suit by The Peace River Manasota Regional Water Supply, Charlotte, Lee and Hardee Counties, as well as the Sierra Club. The lawsuit was unprecedented in Florida history.[15]

As stated earlier, International Mining Corporation, IMC Global, a major fertilizer company, announced that it was merging with Cargill's crop nutrition company. The assets gained from the merger were invested in the new mining operations in Brazil. In a cash and stock purchase, the new Mosaic Company bought the phosphate and potash mining operations of Vale in Brazil.[16] In Florida, they made decisions to run lean and mean, closing down certain operations while continuing to pursue two new mines, one in Manatee County and one in DeSoto County. Both were in the untouched southern extension of the Bone Valley, Hawthorne Group deposits. The Manatee permitting was immediately being challenged in court.

Brazilian potash in 2018 sold for a record $331 a ton, making it far more lucrative than Florida phosphates. In 2011, 165,000 people were employed in Brazilian mining. Brazil's mining exports in that year exceed those in the United States by 27%. Potash, as well as phosphates and other ores, come with potential environmental concerns. No different than Florida phosphate mining, both have waste from the benefication (refining) processes: waste, water consumption and water pollution. These are potential problems only because of the scale of such mining. Vale, which is major stock holder of Mosaic's mining operations, is already involved in two major human and environmental catastrophes resulting from a dam

8.3 Bromadinho, Brazil dam disaster, Alamy.com

breaking at mines they administered in the Minas Gerais (general mining) region of Brazil.. The first dam disaster destroyed the town of Bento Rodrigues in 2015, killing 7 people, injuring many others and forcing an entire village of 500 to move.[17] The water and waste that was released will damage the environment for generations, a fact the company states is not true. The second dam disaster in 2019 killed over 200 people in the town of Brumadinho.[18] (8.3) Vale's stocks plummeted.

Doing their due diligence, *The New York Times* investigated after the two identical disasters, to find how many dams are in the region that were built the same way and how many people are at risk from mining dam failure. The answer is 87 dams with 100,000 people in harm's way. One area of mining operations with three dams now owned by Florida's Mosaic Company is Cajati. In fact, Mosaic's Cajati, Brazil mines and dams lead the story because they pose a high risk to the largest number of people, 11,000.[19] While Mosaic was not responsible for the past dam disasters, I have included these disasters to draw attention to the unintended consequences of large-scale mining. Mosaic, by purchasing the mine and dams at Cajati, is now a part of the problem and not the solution. The three dams they inherited were built exactly like the two that failed.

On October 8, 2008, a headline in the *Sarasota Tribune* read: "Phosphate Mining Challenged by Two Counties."[20] The two counties, Charlotte and Lee, were not the counties where the proposed mines would be or had been permitted. They were down river. The same down river polluted by the pond breech at Fort Meade thirty-five years prior:

> Charlotte and Lee counties, along with a regional water provider, will go to court next week in the latest battle over a proposed 4,200-acre phosphate mine near the Peace River. The Florida Department of Environmental Protection approved the mine site in Hardee County, called Ona, in August 2006. Charlotte and Lee counties and the Peace River/Manasota Regional Water Supply Authority appealed the DEP's approval in state court, claiming the permit did not provide enough protection for the Peace River.

The ink had barely dried on the merger papers that created the new phosphate giant Mosaic, when the permits filed by IMC a decade prior were finally approved by the Hardee County Commissioners resulting in the multi-million-dollar lawsuit. The counties by 2008 had spent $13 million in legal costs. Mosaic's profits for 2008 were $1 billion and they had invested wisely in supporting state elections. Many news services referenced the David v. Goliath nature of the legal action.

At the heart of the lawsuit was the ecology of the entire region. The permitting process and permits, including the required reclamation could not help impacting the wetlands down river in Charlotte and Lee Counties. The fact that the E.P.A. viewed things so narrowly shows that the federal and state enforcement agencies, as well as the environmentalists, have limited knowledge of and concerns for existing eco-systems.

No one should be surprised by this. Just look at the Everglades. The federal and state governments, and their agencies, without understanding the functionality of the northern Everglades to the southern Everglades, spent billions of dollars drying up the land for agricultural use in the northern regions. The 70-year-long tinkering with dams and canals destroyed the Everglades and it will now take trillions of dollars to attempt to restore the entire system. Einstein was right about the infinite amount of human stupidity. After meeting with authority Kevin Erwin, I now believe true reclamation of the central Florida mined area will make the restoration of the Everglades look like a romp through the woods.

Being no match in the legal arena, and with no way to stop the mine, Charlotte and Lee Counties were forced to settle, and Mosaic had to pay in other ways. But the political and business landscape of phosphate mining in the Bone Valley had once again changed dramatically. The opposition did not stop in 2008, it increased. More and more environmental groups began to target Mosaic and Florida phosphate mining in general when the federal government took the giant to court. Certified Senior Ecologist Kevin L. Erwin commented at the time that, "The investment made by Charlotte County, the Peace River Manasota Water Supply Authority and Lee County in challenging IMC Phosphate's permits is significant, but it is small compared to the long-term costs of allowing IMC to strip mine without proper restoration."[21] Erwin has been very outspoken. As described before, he claims that IMC's track record has resulted in improper restoration.

February 2009, in yet another action, groups sued Manatee County and Mosaic over the county's approval of the Altman Tract (8.4). *The Sarasota Herald* reported:

> On behalf of two environmental groups and several residents, Earthjustice is asking the Circuit Court to overturn a County Commission decision to allow Mosaic to mine a 2,048- acre tract commonly called the Altman Tract. That 5-2 vote reversed an earlier decision to deny Mosaic's mining application. The U-turn came after the phosphate giant threatened a $617.8 million lawsuit, based on the value of the land and the phosphate ore beneath it.[22]

8.4 Mosaic's Altman Tract, Manatee County, People Protecting Peace River

The new environmental age, the product of the Nixon administration created to deal with hazardous waste came around decades later to Mosaic's mining practices. On October 1, 2015, *The Tampa Bay Times* wrote:

> Mosaic Fertilizer, the world's largest phosphate mining company, has agreed to pay nearly $2 billion to settle a federal lawsuit over hazardous waste and to clean up operations at six Florida sites and two in Louisiana, the Environmental Protection Agency announced Thursday. The 60 billion pounds of hazardous waste addressed in this case is the largest amount ever covered by a federal or state ... settlement and will ensure that wastewater at Mosaic's facilities is properly managed and does not pose a threat to groundwater resources," the EPA said. The EPA had accused Mosaic of improper storage and disposal of waste from the production of phosphoric and sulfuric acids, key components of fertilizers, at Mosaic's facilities in Bartow, New Wales, Mulberry, Riverview,

South Pierce and Bowling Green in Florida, as well as two sites in Louisiana. The EPA said it had discovered Mosaic employees were mixing highly corrosive substances from its fertilizer operations with the solid waste and wastewater from mineral processing, in violation of federal and state hazardous waste laws.[23]

Since the creation of Mosaic in 2004, the company had invested heavily in public relations. They spent hundreds of thousands yearly supporting local environmental groups. They print beautiful four-color calendars featuring Florida wetlands and wildlife. They have been the face of environmental stewardship and a leader in protecting and restoring the local ecology. Now with the news, they were industrial polluters of the worse kind. The fact that the pollution occurred at all their mines, in the southeast, indicated that it was not accidental, but rather part and parcel of their corporate culture.

March of 2018 was like all the Marches for years as CRU hosted its annual world phosphate conference. Five hundred delegates checked into the Omni Hotel and Resort in Orlando to learn about the projections for the coming months and years for the global phosphate industry and market. The CRU Group specializes in mining, metals and fertilizer commodities, and each year they host a conference in what they refer to as the "heart of the American phosphate industry," But again, there is really only one supplier remaining in Florida, and the signs are clear that they will not be here much longer. Here in Florida, Mosaic paints a picture of a company whose product is critical for feeding the world. In Orlando, they talk about the increasing markets in the United States for vanity, consumer fast foods and power drinks.

The fact is that consumption of phosphates is increasing in the food & beverage industry in carbonated soft drinks, bottled coffee beverages, dairy products, meats, and eggs. The increasing demand for packaged food and beverages owing to convenience and improved shelf life is driving market growth. The global market for food phosphates was worth $480 million to $500 million in 2013 and is growing at an annual rate of roughly 2 percent, estimates Jean Marc Dublanc, vice-president and general manager of Rhodia

Foods North America.[24] But inorganic phosphates now used in many fast foods and drinks in the U.S. may be harmful. Researchers have been studying correlations between phosphate additives and hyperphosphatemia.

Two events in the summer of 2018 may be the death knoll for 135 years of phosphate mining in Bone Valley. On July 26, 2018, residents woke up to a headline in the *Tampa Bay Times*, DeSoto County Commissioners rejected the southern expansion of Mosaic into their county:

> Mosaic Co., the world's largest phosphate company, has spent two decades lining up a new mine in DeSoto County as part of a broader effort to move its operations south. But DeSoto County commissioners last week slammed the door in the company's face, voting 4-1 against rezoning 18,000 acres from agricultural to mining. A major concern: The impact of mining on one of the state's most pristine waterways, Horse Creek. The creek is a major tributary of the Peace River, which supplies water for three counties. The commissioners voted down Mosaic's zoning request Wednesday night after two days of impassioned testimony from hundreds of people opposed to the mine.[25]

The rejection by DeSoto County of the new phosphate mining spoke to the dramatic shift in public opinion. The area was the originating point in 1888 for the phosphate mining boom in central Florida. Central to why, after 135 years of mining phosphates in DeSoto, was the acknowledgement of the true value of their environmental resources. The people had spoken. There was no future for phosphate mining in central Florida, Mosaic was asking too much.

While the temporary loss of the mining opportunity in DeSoto was significant, Mosaic has mines, many mines, and fertilizer plants in four Florida counties. They control all of the phosphate mining in the Bone Valley without a single competitor, which I believe is the textbook definition of a monopoly. Mosaic, of course, immediately appealed the DeSoto County decision in 2019.

Far from the towns and homes around the Peace River, market analysts predict the world phosphate market will be worth $75.17 billion dollars in 2021.[26] The largest growth and market segment will no longer be fertilizers but fast foods. The foods and beverages application is projected to be the fastest growing application in the global phosphate market mainly due to the increasing demand for food. Food grade phosphates are used as food additives owing to properties such as, buffering capacity (pH stabilization), sequestration, and water retention capability. This demand will not be in the United States but rather in the Asian-Pacific regions. In April, 2016, the U.S.D.A. reported that farms switching back to organic operations involved over 21,781 farms and 688,000 acres of farm land. Leading the United States were California and New York. Analysts predict that soon the growth of organic farming will reach double digits.[27] This trend correspondingly reduces the need for phosphate fertilizers by the actual percentage of production by Mosaic in Florida. When Mosaic and the spokespeople for the U.S. phosphate industry praise their efforts, while justifying the many costs to the environment, as feeding the population of the world, they are telling the truth. However, most of us would visualize farm fields with healthy crops. A more accurate picture would be crowds of overweight people eating very un-nutritious fast foods on the go. I have always marveled at the food companies who lose all the vitamins and nutrients processing the foods and then charge you extra to add them back before packaging them for consumers.

The second event in the summer of 2018 was only indirectly involved with Mosaic. A record outbreak of "red tide" appeared in southwest Florida with a record fish kills that lasted into the fall, seriously impacted people's health, marine life, tourism, business and even home sales. The culprit and primary cause was the increased amounts of nutrients entering into rivers and streams flowing into the Gulf. People blamed the state, Mosaic and chemical fertilizers. Personally, my life was so impacted, that I fear future outbreaks.

On September 17, 2018, then Governor Rick Scott, running for U.S. Senate in the November election, was booed out of a Venice

Florida restaurant where he was to hold a campaign event. Here in Charlotte County, during the state-of-emergency, county officials and the tourism department's public relations machinery broke down completely. Their prayers for the red tide to go away were unanswered, Hundreds of thousands of homes sit on the many canals. With each massive fish kill, the dead fish eventually end up in those canals. The push for more mining acres by IMC in the late 1990's had a third track in the southern-most region of Bone Valley, Ona in Hardee County. The last permit was approved January 2, 2019. Hardee County, its commissioners and officials went the way of Manatee County and would not be swayed by environmental concerns like DeSoto County months earlier. Critical to the mining approval was Hillsborough County agreeing to take the waste. The site is now operational and will secure 160.2 million tons of phosphate rock.

In the midst of increasing displays of conflicting interest in the second decade of the twenty-first century. one site to inform the public about the negative outcomes from Florida's phosphate mining, wwwflmines.com, argued against the mining based on *The Public Trust Doctrine*. Familiar with the doctrine from my days in court on the Jersey shore, the author of the article was very astute. The situations involving the Peace and Alafia Rivers, and currently the Santa Fe and New Rivers in Bradford County, can be argued citing the Public Trust Doctrine. The www.flmines.com site states:

> During the past seventy years of phosphate strip mining in west-central Florida, the phosphate industry has at some time been faced with strip mining navigable waterways and riparian lands as defined by "The Public Trust Doctrine." The doctrine defines navigable waterways and riparian lands adjacent to the waterways as public domain.[28]

To take public officials to court and to argue that the officials, based on the doctrine, do not have the 'sovereign authority' "to convey" those waterways and riparian buffer zones to phosphate companies is not only a crap shoot, but a very costly one. Even with legal precedent, as far as I know, a suit involving mining has never been argued using the Public Trust Doctrine.

There is a growing consensus by Florida residents that the risk to the environment posed for allowing new phosphate mining is simply too great. The movement against phosphate mining and mining giant Mosaic has moved beyond the extreme left environmental lobby groups to now incorporate the average resident. Mosaic and defenders of phosphate mining in Florida are losing in the court of public opinion. The major accidents, coupled with the federal lawsuit and settlement have left The Mosaic Company morally bankrupt. "Trust us," simply won't work anymore. Further, to date, Sierra Club and the organized opponents of continued phosphate mining demonstrate that they have yet to discover what this researcher has, that immediately after these new mines are done, Mosaic will be out of here. Another rallying point missed by these environmental groups is the true use of Mosaic's mined phosphates. They would increase their ranks, if the opponents emphasized that the environmental sacrifices are for helping the cattle and meat industries, and not producing healthy food for the world's populations.

While writing this book, I familiarized myself with Mosaic's website. Mosaic's slogan is "We Help the World Grow the Food it Needs." Mosaic continues by highlighting their role in the shift after 3,700 years of farming practices to one using chemical fertilizers to increase crop yields. As stated, and researched, the growth market is for phosphate additives used in processed foods and beverages, not produce farming. The produce farming industry is returning to healthy organic foods.

The World Resource Forum recently addressed the world's limited phosphate reserves, given the growing world population. Citing security needs for those countries that have no reserves, they project that countries will have no other options but to stop importing phosphate rocks and begin using "renewable" phosphate fertilizers such as human excrement. They conclude:

> Although there are ways to recover phosphorus,
> it is clear that we will also have to adopt a more

sustainable approach towards using phosphorus especially as our population is growing- hence food demand will only increase in the future. One way to do so is to encourage diets that contain fewer phosphorus-intensive foods; it is estimated that meat based diets can result in the depletion of up to twice the phosphorus compared to a vegetarian diet.[29]

Another claim by Mosaic and the phosphate industry is that phosphate based-fertilizers account for low food prices. GMOs and pesticide manufactures claim they are the reason. In truth, inflation has had a great deal to do with the most recent decrease. Analysts project the increase demand for meat will increase grain price significantly and will soon cause big increases in food prices

In chapter I, I covered the work by the fathers of organic farming. Sir Albert Howard learned first-hand in the third-world and densely populated country of India that their traditional methods of farming were superior to the new scientific methods. Eighty years later, his conclusions have been repeatedly confirmed. In terms of the environmental outcomes from both agricultural processes and the reliance on phosphate fertilizers, both were negligible at the time he conducted his work. Today the impact on the environment from the increase in the scale of both farm lands and mining lands, as well as the waste and unintended consequences, cannot be ignored.

ENDNOTES

[1] *New York Times*, June 11,1978. https://www.nytimes.com/1978/06/11/archives/florida-battling-phosphate-industry- over-mining.html

[2] Leah Holst, paper, 2018

[3] T.D. Allman, 2013

[4] Kirkpatrick Sale, 2000

[5] T.D. Allman, 2013

[6] Kevin Erwin, "The Cost of Reclamation, The Price of Failure," Editorial, Tampa, FL, *The Tampa Bay Tribune*, May 3, 2004

[7] *Ibid.*

[8] *Ibid.*

[9] Interview with Kevin Erwin, March 2019

[10] Florida Sierra Club, https://www.sierraclub.org/florida/phosphate-mining

[11] *Ibid.*

[12] *Ibid.*

[13] *Ibid.*

[14] Protectpeaceriver.org, A New Mosaic Agreement, website, May 5, 2019

[15] USGS study 1990s diminishing phosphate reserves

[16] *Charlotte Sun Herald*, "A united front beneficial when fighting phosphate," March 6, 2009

[17] en.wikipedia.org/wiki/Bento_Rodrigues_dam_disaster

[18] *The Guardian*, "Brazil dam collapse: 10 bodies found and hundreds missing," Jan. 25, 2019

[19] *New York Times* "Why Did the Dam in Brazil Collapse? Here's A Brief Look," Jan. 25, 2019

[20] *Sarasota Tribune*, "Phosphate Mining Challenged by Two Counties," October 8, 2008

[21] *Ibid.*

[22] *Sarasota Herald,* "Lawsuit Altman Tract," DeSoto, 2009

[23] *Tampa Bay Times*, October 1, 2015

[24] https://www.icis.com/explore/resources/news/2000/11/13/126148/food-phosphates-market-restructures/

[25] *Tampa Bay Times*, July 26, 2018

[26] https://www.powershow.com/view0/8dfb43-MjhjM/Phosphate_Market_-Regional_Trends_Forecast_to_2021_powerpoint_ppt_presentation

[27] https://kohalacenter.org/archive/laulima/pdf/OAIG_OrgAgRetrospective.pdf

[28] www.flmines.com

[29] https://phosphorusalliance.org/2018/12/the-phosphorus-sustainability-challenge/

IX.

EPILOGUE,
SEARCHING FOR QUESTIONS

"All the king's horses, and all the king's men, could
not put poor Humpty Dumpty back together again."

Nursery Rhyme

It was almost the first day of spring, 2019, when I drove down to
Fort Myers to meet with Kevin Erwin. Living in Florida only a
brief time now, I am still aware of the signs of the changing seasons.
No different from the north, certain trees and shrubs burst in color,
announcing the advent of spring. For such a seemingly predictable
landscape, if one takes the time to fully live in here, there are a
multitude of surprises.

Erwin, an ecologist, who has spent a lifetime studying the ecology
of Florida, has a small consulting company of one. His offices are
in a small former home, not far from the Caloosahatchee River in
downtown Fort Myers. When I visited with him, he announced that
he was moving his offices into his home and donating the present
building to be a shelter for homeless mothers. I arranged to meet
Erwin because if there is anything you need to know about the effects
of phosphate mining on the Florida environment, he is the most
qualified person to consult. After all my work researching for this
book, I had concluded that despite the peak of phosphate mining
being reached, the epoch was far from over. There will be the long
process of restoring the land, if that is even possible. Like so many, I

went searching for answers. Within minutes of our meeting, Erwin brought me to the true nature of the problem. What is required now, and as quickly as possible, is the search for questions.

I was asked to speak on bioregionalism in the Soviet Union in 1990, only a few years after the Chernobyl reactor accident. To date, Chernobyl is considered the worse man-made disaster in human history. A new science was born in its aftermath, due to the fact that what resulted from the fire and meltdown has never existed prior. Therefore, in terms of nature, the products of the accident were unknown. I bring up Chernobyl because after 135 years of phosphate mining in Florida, when the companies fill in the mines and execute the now legally required reclamation of the particular ecology, there is a totally different environment.

The result is man-made and in almost all situations done without a proper analysis and mapping of what was there before. While today, bioregionalism is a relic of the early Green Party, I still believe in its contributions as a philosophy and practice as related in Kirkpatrick Sale's book on the subject, *Dwellers in the Land*. As a practice, it has us live in place and not in generalizations about environment.

In Chapter II, I wrote about the particular mix,[1] that exists in a given area that contains either phosphate pebbles or phosphate rock at a certain depth below and next to other deposits. The mix is a critical determinant as to the feasibility of mining the phosphates, as well as the depth and degrees of waste.[2] Unique to Florida and all other phosphate areas on the planet is the nature of the landscape beginning as the raised ocean floor. The limestone serving as the crust of a pizza with millions of years of toppings, layers of different deposits, (primarily sand, clays and other minerals), and some 15 to 30 feet of overburden.[3] Erwin is quick to draw attention to the immense size in acres of the lands in Florida that have been dug up and then filled in, some 450,000 acres according to Florida's Department of Environmental Protection. If you view a map it is an area that is close to one-third of the state, smack in the middle of the peninsula (9.1). It was surprising to visualize. Now I know the nature of the problem going forward is the lack of questions being asked by the state officials, the E.P.A., the county officials, and even the environmentalists.

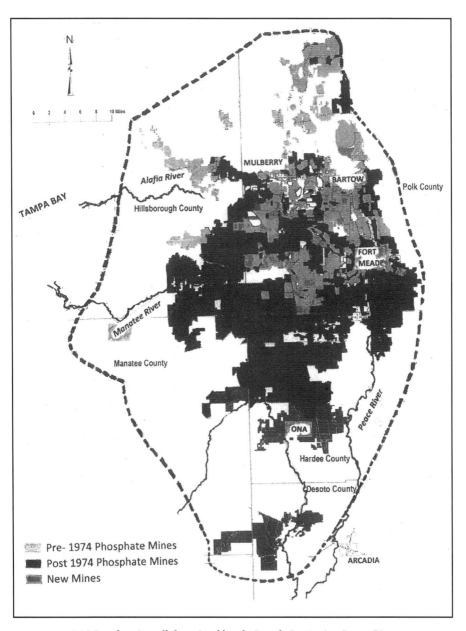

9.1 Map showing all the mined lands, People Protecting Peace River

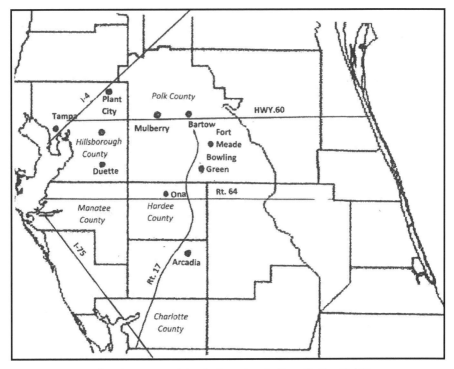

9.2 Map showing present Mosaic Co. mines in Bone Valley, Ted Ehmann

What we have in one third of the state of Florida is an entire region that has been filled back in with a mix of layers, a mix that was not there before, a mix that not does resemble or function as the prior mix. I have kept the simple quote by Wendell Berry close to me since first reading it in 1989. In the middle portion of Florida men with machines and an "inadequate culture" have shaken things up.[4] In almost all cases, they never questioned what was there before the strip mining. (9.2) They never made a map so they could find their way back. Truth be told, the officials and environmental specialists had no knowledge of how the ecology in that area functioned as a whole. Sure, they have known for decades the parts, but not the whole; not the relationships between the parts, the systems. It was, even though they did not question an observable living system. What has replaced it? Now that they have mixed everything up and thrown it back on top of the crust, how well will the new man-made system function. In Chapter I, I began this journey into the mining of phosphate for agriculture, which according to a leading authority on organic farming, is in its very nature counter to viewing the land as a living system.[5]

Then there are all those tracts of abandoned strip mining from the years before the age of environmentalism. Those lands are a dysfunctional part of a larger system. (9.3) Now they are vacant, useless and lifeless. What will be the impact on having whole areas of an ecology rendered useless? Around Chernobyl, they have been asking this question for thirty-two years now.

One thing we do have a knowledge of in Florida, is it has a rich history of such recklessness. The same officials that created the disaster called the new Everglades, are the same people in charge of the reclamation of the strip-mined regions. These authorities approved and went forward with drying up the northern lands for farming and development. We know seventy years later that they never cared to ask how the ecology of the Everglades worked. Now it will require billions of dollars to restore the natural system, if that is even remotely possible. Scientist remain hopeful, but many feel it is too little, too late. The Comprehensive Everglades Restoration Plan, while noble, is still a government funded project and like all government funded programs, the funds can disappear.[6] At issue with the restoration of lands in Bone Valley mined after 1987, the responsibility falls on the mining company with oversight by the government. The reality of company mandated restoration was talked about by Wendell Berry way back in 1977: "In practice, the economic and political power that accompanies large size provides a constant temptation to the large firm to take the benefits and pass on the costs."

Decades after the United Nations designated the Florida Everglades as a World Heritage Site, the Everglades became the first of such sites to earn the recognition of being "in danger." The costs so far, as of the close of 2019, has been 7 billion dollars. Authorities state that even now, they are unsure if they can restore the Everglades. We have no idea what it would take to restore all the exploited lands in Bone Valley, perhaps hundreds of billions

9.3 *View of repaired sink hole, Florida Department of Enviromental Protection*

of dollars. One thing is sure, the benefits of supplying the world's phosphates for fertilizers are not the state of Florida's, but the costs will be ours for generations.

There are also the unforeseen costs of mining phosphate in Florida, as the sink hole accident at Mosaic's Mulberry facility will attest to. That cost is the company's. To give a sense of the scale of mining and the corresponding scale of accidents, an executive told *Reuters* in 2016[7] that it would cost the company between 20 to 50 million dollars to fix the sink hole.

The *Ledger.com* reported on May 30, 2018 that the cost ended being 84 million dollars, a difference of 34 Million. (9.3) Folks like Kevin Erwin will attest to decades of misquoted reclamation costs, always in the company's favor and to the detriment of thousands of mined acres.

My meeting with Kevin Erwin was profound. Erwin has spent his entire career researching and addressing the problem. He admits that after all those years, he has more questions than answers. He believes the most important question to ask is what is happening, and what will happen below the surface. He already knows the problems on the surface, with growing things and the quality of the surface waters after decades of improper reclamation by mining companies. Key to that aftermath is the permeability of the returned mix. When the clays are mixed haphazardly with the sands and other layers, citrus groves, trees and shrubs cannot properly root and drink. But what about below that?

What defines the geology of Florida is the water. Below is the huge aquifer fed by hundreds, even thousands of springs.[8] Above ground, due to the flatness of the interior, Florida has large sheets of extremely slow-moving surface water. In contrast, far below are fast moving rivers of pristine spring water. What the men and their machine culture have put in between the ground water and the aquifer, has never existed there before. Yet, the parties concerned, all act as if they know what is going on.

Driving home from my meeting, I kept thinking about the need for more Kevin Erwin, how to clone him. He confirmed at age 67, he intended to work till he drops. He also stated that he has made arrangements to donate all his papers and work to Florida Gulf Coast University. Erwin intends someday to publish a book on his work. However, a force of one, he appears unable to manage his work without the added industry of writing a book. No matter what happened in the next ten years, Erwin's files, data, photographs and papers are the closest thing to a map we have for going forward. It is, as well, the correct mindset to reclaim and restore Florida; the asking of the right questions.

Two years after my interview with Kevin Erwin, a website *class action reporter*[9] reported on a large land class action law suit against four developers in Polk County in May of 2020. The class action suit has to do with previous mined lands in Polk County, specifically the strip-mined areas around Angler's Green and Paradise Lakes, properties mined by Mosaic Co. after 1975 and subject to the restorative reclamation laws in Florida. Lots were sold by developers for homes who had purchased the supposed properly reclaimed lands there from Mosaic. First the plaintiffs assert that the Mosaic is liable for they contaminated the properties by "improperly managing and disposing of radioactive mining wastes." The plaintiffs go on to address the very issue and red flag about reclamation that has been Kevin Erwin's work.

> Under Florida law, mining companies are required to restore former mining lands in a manner that returns the land to its original condition prior to mining waste disposal or mining operations.

The Complaint cites internal agency documents that government scientists noted with "significant concern":

> The use of slag as a fill resulting in contamination with elevated concentrations of decay products of uranium, including radium-226 in the soils of the previously mined areas. That radium-226 and other substances produce gamma radiation that can increase risks of cancer, including leukemia, lymphoma and thyroid cancer. Since the half-life of radium-226 is 1,600 years, the risk will be there if not decontaminated for sixteen centuries.[10]

The experts also state that decay of radium creates radon. I know that issue personally from living up north and trying to sell a property that tested for radon. Scientist have long shown that the gas can increase the risk of lung cancer.

As more and more people look to buy a home in paradise, and in this case the center wilderness corridor of Florida, they often encounter fraud and misrepresentation, nothing new to Florida development schemes. I recently spent time talking to a couple whose son bought a house in Hillsborough County, only to find out that they had purchased the house, but the land was still owned by the phosphate mining giant, Mosaic Company.

In this book, I have strived to give an accurate account of a hitherto unfamiliar, yet important history. That it may guide future generations to act wisely in all areas of exploitation of both our precious lands and communities, is my fervent wish.

ENDNOTES

[1] Florida Department of Environment Protection, https://floridadep.gov/water/mining-mitigation/content/phosphate F.I.P.R. Institute, www.fipr.state.fl.us/about-us/phosphate-primer/florida-phosphate-mining-history/

[2] *Ibid.*

[3] *Ibid.*

[4] Wendell Berry, *What Are People For?*, 2010

[5] Eliot Coleman, *The New Organic Grower*, 1995

[6] https://floridadep.gov/eco-pro/eco-pro/content/comprehensive-everglades-restoration-plan-cerp

[7] Reuters, August, 2017

[8] Coastgis.marsci.uga.edu/summit/aquifers_fla.htm

[9] https://classactionsreporter.com/mosaic-co-phosphate-mining-contamination-florida-land-class-actio

[10] *Ibid.*

BIBLIOGRAPHY

Agricultural Society of South Carolina, *Memorial to Dr. St. Julien Ravenel*, Charleston, SC, 1882

Allman, T.D., *Finding Florida, The True History of the Sunshine State,* New York, NY, Grove Press, 2013

Berry, Wendell, *The Unsettling of America: Culture and Agriculture,* Counterpoint, 2015

_____, *What Are People For?,* Counterpoint, 2010

Brown, Canter Jr., *Florida's Peace River Frontier*, Orlando, FL, University Press of Central Florida, 1991

Capra, Fritjob, *The Turning Point, Science, Society and the Rising Culture,* New York, NY, Bantam Books, 1982

Chazal, Philip E., *The Century In Phosphates and Fertilizers,* Charleston, SC, 1904

Cook, David, "Dunn tells how he got into mining business," *Ocala Star Banner,* February 19, 2011

Dinkins, J. Lester, *Dunnellon Boomtown of the 1890's,* self-published, 1969

Erwin, Kevin, "The Cost of Reclamation, The Price of Failure," Editorial, Tampa, FL, *The Tampa Bay Tribune*, May 3, 2004

_____, *An Analysis of IMC Reclamation Costs For the Proposed Ona Mine,* Report, 2004

Florida Industrial Phosphate Research Institute Website, www.fipr.state.fl.us

Gunset, George, "IMC Global to Cutback In Phosphate Sector," *Chicago Tribune*, November 12, 1999

Holst, Leah, *The Impact of Environmental Activism on Phosphate Mining in Florida: From Bone Valley to the Gulf Coast, 1911 – 1992,* April 10, 2018

Howard, Albert, *An Agricultural Testament*, London, England, Oxford University Press, 1940

Jasinski, Richard, Reports USGS, ww.usgs.gov/centers/nmic/phosphate-rock-statistics-and-information

King, Wayne, "Florida's Phosphate Pollution Stirs Alarm*," New York Times*, July 24,1976

Mazoyer, Marcel and Laurence Roudart, *A History of World Agriculture from the Neolithic age to the current crisis,* New York, NY, Earthscan, 2006

McKinley, Shepherd W., *Stinking Stones and Rocks of Gold: Phosphate, Fertilizer and Industrialization in South Carolina,* Gainesville, FL, The University Press of Florida, 2017

Melr, Rinde, *Richard Nixon and the Rise of American Environmentalism,* Science & History Org., June 2, 2017

Mosaic Company Website, www.mosaicco.com

New York Times, "Florida Battling Phosphate Mining Companies Over Disputed Lands*,"* July 11, 1978

Pittman, Craig, *Tampa Bay Times*, October 1, 2015

_____, "Mosaic spent 20 years planning a new phosphate mine, DeSoto has rejected it," *Tampa Bay Times*, July 26, 2018

Randazzo, Anthony F., Jones, Douglas S, *The Geology of Florida,* University Press of Florida, 1997

Sale, Kirkpatrick, *Dwellers In The Land, The Bioregional Vision, University of Georgia Press*, 2000

_____, *Human Scale*, Chelsea Green Publishing, 2017

Second Agricultural Revolution, secondagriculturalrevolution. weebly.com/impact.html

Shepard, Mark, *Restoration Agriculture,* Acres U.S.A., 2013

Shuler, Krisria A., Bailey. Jr., Ralph, *A History of the Phosphate Mining Industry in the South Carolina Lowlands,* Mount Pleasant, SC, 2004

Stephens, Lester D., *Ancient Animals and Wondrous Things, The Story of Francis Simmons Holmes*, Charleston, SC, Charleston Museum, n.d.

Trinkley, Michael, "South Carolina Land Phosphates In the Late Nineteenth and Early Twentieth Centuries, Toward An Archaeological Context," chicora.org

Turner, Gregg M., *A Journey into Florida Railroad History,* University Press of Florida, 2008

Wise, Stephen R. and Lawrence S. Rowland, *Rebellion, Reconstruction and Redemption 1861-1893*, Columbia, SC, University of South Carolina Press, 2015

ABOUT THE AUTHOR

TED EHMANN was born in Trenton, New Jersey in 1949. He took to fine art at an early age. attending the Philadelphia College of Art to study painting. Many years later, he returned to college and earned his BFA, going on to earn his masters in teaching history from the College of New Jersey. Beginning in 1989, besides teaching, he traveled extensively, connecting to and painting nature and wilderness. He studied Bioregionalism and founded Penn's Valley Greens, organizing regional yearly conferences and sharing this new ecological viewpoint as far as the Soviet Union.

Upon moving to Florida in 2016, he pursued his life-long interest in prehistory and history and nature, authoring in 2020, *The People of the Great Circle*, which detailed the incredible twenty-five century long prehistory of the mound building Indians in South Florida. In January Ehmann's *Charlotte County Florida , a History,* his unvarnished retelling of the people and places that still impact the South Gulf Coast county today, was published for the centennial there.

Boom & Bust in Bone Valley is another history of forgotten Florida that chronicles 135 years of phosphate mining in Florida, and the looming ecological crisis in his newly adopted home. This history, provides the author the opportunity to return to his roots as a bioregionalist in the Delaware Valley thirty years ago while exposing the deadly consequences of massive strip mining in his adopted state over time.

INDEX

A

accidents, xii, 25, 35, 150, 160

agri-businesses, 18

agricultural revolution, vii, 1, 9, 17

agriculture, ii, vii, 1, 4-8, 10-13, 17-20, 44, 57-58, 109, 122, 131, 159

Alachua County, 52

Altman Tract, 144-145, 153

American Cyanamid, 114, 117-120

aquifer, 36, 130, 137, 140, 161

Arcadia Phosphate Company, 99

Audubon Society, 124

B

Bartow, FL, v, xiii, 5, 88, 90-91, 93, 104, 116, 120, 129-130, 145

Beaufort County, S.C, 5, 41, 45-46, 51, 96, 105, 114

beneficiation, 32, 112, 127, 34, 38, 124

Berry, Wendell, i, v, xiii, 8-12, 16, 21-23, 28, 158-159, 163

Berthier, Pierre, 3

bioregionalism, 109, 132, 156, 164

Boca Grande FL, 60, 67, 69-70

Bone Valley, ii, iv-viii, xii-xiii, 3, 5, 20-21, 25-26, 28-29, 31, 36, 40, 42, 44, 47, 49, 51-52, 62-64, 71, 79-85, 87-88, 90-92, 96, 109, 111, 113-115, 118, 120, 122-123, 125, 127-129, 131, 135-137, 141, 144, 147, 149, 158-159, 164

Brewster mining town, 114

C

Cedar Key, FL, 68-69

Charlotte County, 80, 122, 144, 148, 164

clay, 28, 33-35, 39, 52, 122, 125-126, 139

convict labor, 64, 66

crops, xii, 1, 9-10, 13, 15-18, 21, 44, 55, 98, 115, 148

D

Desoto County, FL, xii, 77, 83-85, 91, 99, 141, 147, 149

DeSoto County, xii, 77, 83-85, 91, 99, 141, 147, 149

Disston, Hamilton, 56-57, 83

dragline, 30-31, 109, 111-112

Dunnellon Phosphate Company, 51, 102

Dunn, John F., 96-99, 101-105

Dunnellon, FL, 31, 33, 42, 45-46, 51-53, 64, 69, 101-102, 104-105

Marion County, FL, 62, 97-99, 101, 105
Mark Shepherd, 19
mix, vii, 25, 28, 37, 96, 139-140, 156, 158, 161
Mosaic Company, v, x, xii, 118, 123, 129, 141-142, 150, 162
Mulberry, FL, iii, xii, 36-37, 47, 92, 118, 120, 129-130, 145, 160
Mulberry sink hole, 129

N

National Environmental Policy Act, 122
Nichols, mining town, 120
Nixon, Richard M., 121-123, 144
Noralyn plant, 130-131

P

Page, John W., 47, 90, 101, 111
peak phosphorus, 8
permaculture, 18
phosphogypsum, 36-37, 126
phosphoric acid, 36, 111, 126
Plant, Henry B, ii, iv, x, 3-4, 7, 12-13, 17, 30, 32, 34-37, 57-59, 62, 64, 67-68, 71-73, 84, 106, 110, 129-131, 137
Polk County, FL, v, 42, 47-49, 80, 83-84, 88, 90, 92, 101, 116, 125, 161
Port Inglis, 63, 69

R

radium, 162
reclamation, 20, 56, 82, 122-123, 126-129, 137-141, 143-144, 152, 156, 159-161
red tide, xi-xii, 19, 148-149
riparian buffers, 19
Roosevelt, Franklin D, 18, 72, 115-116
Roosevelt, Theodore, 18, 72, 115-116

S

Sale, Kirkpatrick, v, 2, 6-7, 21-22, 109, 116, 122, 132, 136, 152, 156, 171
Scott, George W., 99-100, 102, 104, 148
Shepard, Mark, 13, 18-19
Sierra Club, 124, 131, 140-141, 150, 152
soil fertility, 7, 11, 17, 52-53, 115-116
Southern Extension Zone Bone Valley, 29
Steiner, Rudolph, 7, 17-18
sustainability, 7, 68, 129, 153

T

Tampa Bay, 42, 58, 64, 68, 71, 73, 76, 130, 145, 147, 152-153

U

United States Geologic Survey, 41

V

Vogt, Augustus, 44, 97-99, 101,
104-105
Von Liebig, Justus, 1-3

Available From Shotwell Publishing

If you enjoyed this book, perhaps some of our other titles will pique your interest. The following titles are now available for your reading pleasure... Enjoy!

MARK C. ATKINS

WOMEN IN COMBAT
Feminism Goes to War

JOYCE BENNETT

MARYLAND, MY MARYLAND
The Cultural Cleansing of a Small Southern State

GARRY BOWERS

SLAVERY AND THE CIVIL WAR
What Your History Teacher Didn't Tell You

DIXIE DAYS
Reminiscences Of A Southern Boyhood

JERRY BREWER

DISMANTLING THE REPUBLIC

ANDREW P. CALHOUN, JR.

MY OWN DARLING WIFE
Letters from a Confederate Volunteer

JOHN CHODES

SEGREGATION
Federal Policy or Racism?

WASHINGTON'S KKK
The Union League during Southern Reconstruction

WALTER BRIAN CISCO

WAR CRIMES AGAINST SOUTHERN CIVILIANS

PAUL C. GRAHAM

CONFEDERAPHOBIA
An American Epidemic

WHEN THE YANKEES COME
Former South Carolina Slaves Remember Sherman's Invasion

T.L. HULSEY

25 TEXAS HEROES

JOSEPH JAY

SACRED CONVICTION
The South's Stand for Biblical Authority

SUZANNE PARFITT JOHNSON

MAXCY GREGG'S SPORTING JOURNALS 1842 - 1858

JAMES RONALD KENNEDY

DIXIE RISING: Rules for Rebels

WHEN REBEL WAS COOL
Growing Up in Dixie, 1950-1965

JAMES R. & WALTER D. KENNEDY

PUNISHED WITH POVERTY
The Suffering South – Prosperity to Poverty and the Continuing Struggle

THE SOUTH WAS RIGHT!

YANKEE EMPIRE
Aggressive Abroad and Despotic at Home

PHILIP LEIGH

CAUSES OF THE CIVIL WAR

THE DEVIL'S TOWN
Hot Springs During the Gangster Era

U.S. GRANT'S FAILED PRESIDENCY

LEWIS LIBERMAN

SNOWFLAKE BUDDIES
ABC Leftism for Kids!

JACK MARQUARDT

AROUND THE WORLD
IN EIGHTY YEARS
Confessions of a Connecticut
Confederate

MICHAEL MARTIN

SOUTHERN GRIT
Sensing the Siege at Petersburg

SAMUEL W. MITCHAM

THE GREATEST LYNCHING IN
AMERICAN HISTORY: New York, 1863

CHARLES T. PACE

LINCOLN AS HE REALLY WAS

SOUTHERN INDEPENDENCE.
WHY WAR?
The War to Prevent Southern
Independence

JAMES RUTLEDGE ROESCH

FROM FOUNDING FATHERS
TO FIRE EATERS
The Constitutional Doctrine of
States' Rights in the Old South

KIRKPATRICK SALE

EMANCIPATION HELL
The Tragedy Wrought by Lincoln's
Emancipation Proclamation

KAREN STOKES

A LEGION OF DEVILS
Sherman in South Carolina

CAROLINA LOVE LETTERS

JACK TROTTER

LAST TRAIN TO DIXIE

LESLIE R. TUCKER

OLD TIMES THERE SHOULD
NOT BE FORGOTTEN
Cultural Genocide in Dixie

JOHN VINSON

SOUTHERNER, TAKE YOUR STAND!
Reclaim Your Identity. Reclaim your Life.

HOWARD RAY WHITE

HOW SOUTHERN FAMILIES
MADE AMERICA
Colonization, Revolution, and Expansion
From Virginia Colony to the Republic
of Texas 1607 to 1836

UNDERSTANDING CREATION
AND EVOLUTION

ANNE WILSON SMITH

ROBERT E. LEE:
A History Book for Kids

DR. CLYDE N. WILSON

LIES MY TEACHER TOLD ME
The True History of the War
for Southern Independence
& Other Essays

THE OLD SOUTH
50 Essential Books
(Southern Reader's Guide 1)

THE WAR BETWEEN THE STATES
60 Essential Books
(Southern Reader's Guide 2)

RECONSTRUCTION AND
THE NEW SOUTH, 1865-1913
50 Essential Books
(Southern Reader's Guide 3)

THE SOUTH 20TH CENTURY
AND BEYOND
50 Essential Books
(Southern Reader's Guide 4)

THE YANKEE PROBLEM
An American Dilemma
(The Wilson Files 1)

NULLIFICATION
Reclaiming the Consent of the
Governed
(The Wilson Files 1I)

ANNALS OF THE STUPID PARTY
Republicans Before Trump
(The Wilson Files 1II)

JOE A. WOLVERTON, II

"WHAT DEGREE OF MADNESS?"
Madison's Method to Make
American STATES Again

WALTER KIRK WOOD

BEYOND SLAVERY
The Northern Romantic Nationalist
Origins of America's Civil War

GREEN ALTAR BOOKS
(Literary Imprint)

CATHARINE SAVAGE BROSMAN

AN AESTHETIC EDUCATION
and Other Stories

CHAINED TREE, CHAINED OWLS:
Poems

RANDALL IVEY

A NEW ENGLAND ROMANCE
and Other SOUTHERN Stories

JAMES EVERETT KIBLER

TILLER

THOMAS MOORE

A FATAL MERCY
The Man Who Lost The Civil War

KAREN STOKES

BELLES
A Carolina Love Story

CAROLINA TWILIGHT

HONOR IN THE DUST

THE IMMORTALS

THE SOLDIER'S GHOST
A Tale of Charleston

WILLIAM A. THOMAS, JR.

RUNAWAY HALEY
An Imagined Family Saga

GOLD-BUG

MICHAEL ANDREW GRISSOM

BILLIE JO

BRANDI PERRY

SPLINTERED
A New Orleans Tale

MARTIN L. WILSON

TO JEKYLL AND HIDE

Free Book Offer

Sign-up for new release notifications and receive a **FREE** downloadable edition of *Lies My Teacher Told Me: The True History of the War for Southern Independence* by Dr. Clyde N. Wilson and *Confederaphobia: An American Epidemic by* Paul C. Graham by visiting FreeLiesBook.com. You can always unsubscribe and keep the book, so you've got nothing to lose!

Made in the USA
Columbia, SC
24 July 2021